Spear Masters

A Historical Survey of The Minds of African Warrior Scholars Vol. 4

By: Kofi Piesie Research Team

© Same Tree Different Branch Publishing

All right reserved. No part of this book may be reproduced or transmitted in any form or by any means, electronic or mechanical, including photocopying, recording, or by any information storage and retrieval systems without the written permission of the publisher.

Printed in the United States of America

We, the Spear Masters, would like to welcome you to Kofi Piesie Research Team fourth volume, and by the end of this publication, we hope you, the reader knows who the Dinka are and how important the spear, our livestock, and our will to fight for our survival. We also hope each survey you read is a valuable lesson and something you can take, share, and possibly apply.

We, the Spears Masters, would like the reader to pay attention to the full title of this publication, which is Spear Masters: A Historical Survey of The Minds of African Warrior Scholars Vol 4. The subtitle is what people tend to miss, meaning these are SURVEYS in the minds of African Warrior Scholars. A survey is a research method used to collect data from a predefined group of respondents to gain information and insights into various topics of interest.

Table Content

Foreward - Mkuu Mzee

Introduction - Kofi Piesie

Part I (Dinka)

Survey One – The Dinka by: Kofi Piesie

Survey Two – Lot Boys of Sudan by: Kofi Piesie

Survey Three – John Garang The Dinka Leader by: Kofi Piesi

Part II (Combat)

Survey Four – Surveying the Spear Masters by: T'challa Bangoura

Part III (History)

Survey Five - AAVE & Code Switching: Products of the Influence Acculturation and Assimilation by: Chavis Tp-hsb Ahaw McCray

Survey Six - Sun Worship: Expanded Sun Gods by: Setepenre Meri Amen

Part IV (As I Learn We All Learn)

Survey Seven - The Legend of 'Alī Bēr Shī' Alī Sunnī' Alī (1464-92) by: Ini-Herit Shawn P

Survey Eight - Morocco, Ahmad al-Mansur & The Demise of Songhai by: Sutekh Akande Iyanu-Oluwa

Part V (Culture)

Survey Nine - A Warrior-Scholar Examination and Assessment of African American/African Biblical Religious belief via the use of Psychology, Sociology, Epistemology & Hermeneutics by Chavis Tp-hsb Ahaw McCray

Acknowledgment

Sutekh Akande Iyanu-Oluwa Acknowledgements

For me, this volume is dedicated to all supporters of Kofi Piesie Research Team and Mossi Warrior Clan. Also, to Black Pantha for the work that you have put in to bring the accurate information about Africa and its cultures and Kimoyo to the people. All the hard work you do is definitely appreciated and valued. To Ankh West, who shouts out the team at every opportunity. Thank you for setting the blueprint that we continue to follow. You revolutionized my thinking as well as the conscious community. You are our number one supporter. To everyone that enjoys African and African American history and culture. Spears are flying, and pseudos are crying!

Acknowledgment

Ini-Herit (Shawn P)

I would like to dedicate this book to my family and friends who have been with us throughout this journey and the young women and men who will find themselves learning from our work and the history of our ancestors. I would like to dedicate this book to you, the reader, as well as Juan Vasquez, Nunu, Juju, CK, Cheetah, Amber Willis, and your children for allowing us to be a part of your growth and development. To everyone that has subscribed to Science w/ Shawn and the families who continue to push us forward and provide us with an opportunity to follow in the footsteps of our ancestors.

Acknowledgment

Chavis Tp-hsb Ahaw McCray

Acknowledgments In this journey, we call life my wife, who birthed my children, has been with me through my extreme highs and extreme lows and deserves the first acknowledgment. Though my love for knowledge and reading worked her nerves many days, I know the manifestation of my ideas to physical form excites her just as much as me. I appreciate her for being the first person to advise me to think about writing something with all these new things I was learning. Our situation motivated me to make something out of nothing and show her none of this educating myself was a waste of time. If anyone has had to put up with my growth and changes in perspective, it's her. There were times where things got rough due to my unsubscribing to Christianity, yet on 7/24 we will have been married 6 years and together 10+ yrs. Thank you for being the Ryder I always knew you were and having my babies who motivated me to be something better than I was. I thank my momma and Aunt Lisa for the strongest encouragement and best support a person could have. I always wanted to make both of you proud of my intellect, and now I'm getting that chance to take that opportunity. I thank my brothers Chad and Chase for the love and support, and momma used to tell us we all we got. I want to acknowledge my granny, the greatest woman walking this planet in my eyes. There is no one more dependable or caring than Verda Belle. Only Big mama Ella Johnson comes close. These women are the wisest I know and deserve recognition. I acknowledge my father for making me read them Encyclopedia volumes, memorize bible books, making me do current events, and being my biggest critic. I thank you for the inspiration through false ideas you had of me not liking to read. I want to thank my aunt Val who always knew I was intelligent and capable of things beyond my imagination. I want to acknowledge my Papa James "Duke" McCray, who showed me what a father and a man of integrity was, along with my father, who help mold the foundation to create the man I am today. I appreciate your death revealing to me exactly what a legacy was and putting fire in my butt to start leaving a legacy of my own. I acknowledge all the McCrays, Hawkins, Thealls, Slaughter, Perkins, and long live Marlon Gomez while I'm at its free JD, BG, Binky.

I thank KOFI for giving me an opportunity and a platform to learn from him and take to utilize on my own for later. I acknowledge Shawn for keeping my steel sharper than a ginsu blade. I appreciate Sutekh for your role in me jumping down with KPRT. I appreciate the leveling up in the stock game from Setepenre and wisdom of Tchalla. All y'all gave me a lane to do something productive with my life and legacy in adding me to the team, and I am forever grateful. I appreciate Harold Johnson for being a behind the scenes big homie giving me books and Ankh West and Wudjau Iry Maat for being ambassadors of scientific literacy.

Their examples of great teachers I soaked up game from to build my warrior scholar reasoning and intellectual arsenal. Shout out to my fb friends NuNu and Juju y'all Know who y'all are. Shout out Mike Rainey, Big Cliff, Felipe (Flop Po) Mav Monk, Raheem, Chris, and Seth Hunter; the whole Scarborough 2005 varsity basketball team shout out Robert Rann. Shout out to my supervisor Danny and co-worker Donny boy. Shout out Braden Marshall, Jus Bates, my lil cousins Darrel and Darrien, all they sisters. Shout out to the lil homie Marquez Boyd, Deneshia, Yahara, and anybody else that seen me come up from nothing and showed love I hope this work is edifying and cherished as I put my all into it.

Acknowledgment

Setepenre Meri Amen

I would like to Acknowledge the oldest book in the world "The Teachings of Ptahhotep" the very first passage in the book speaks of one not being arrogant when we gain knowledge. Coming into this thing we call "The conscious community" we find out things we were not taught in school about our black history. We want to attack people with misinformation, but we must be humble and share the knowledge for there is much to learn from the wise and the ignorant alike.

"Do not be proud and arrogant with your knowledge. Consul and converse with the ignorant and with wise, for the limits of the art are not reached. No artist ever possesses that perfection to which he should aspire." - The Teachings of Ptahhotep

Acknowledgment

Kofi Piesie

First and foremost, I would like to thank my Ancestors who came before me. Jerreh len jeff suma ai maai mi contan si yen torop.(Honor our Ancestors, and we respect you and proud of things you've done. I want to thank the team, the Kofi Piesie Research Team, for you all hard work and dedication. I want to also thank the mighty, mighty Mossi Warrior Clan for continuing to inspire me. Salute to everyone who has supported each volume. I greatly appreciate you all.

Acknowledgment

T'challa Bangoura

To every living organism that manifested, reproduced, and died to ultimately evolve into our species. To every human that risked and sacrificed their lives to preserve our species.To the countless Afrikans that have been and are continuously being murdered in cold blood to this very day.To each and every one of you that find yourselves reading these acknowledgments in your continued support of the Kofi Piesie Research Team, I am eternally grateful. For it not for all of the above-mentioned events, energy, and people, we would not be here doing what we love. It is a great honor to attain knowledge; it is an obligation to share that knowledge. That is part of gaining wisdom. I am grateful for those that continue to impart knowledge on me, and I hope to do my part and participate in the reciprocation process. Although my foundation as a child growing up here in Chicago(and a few years in California) was Baptist Christian, I have been able to expand my horizon and uncover many gems of not just Afrika, but the world. Many say "it's a small world" but truthfully it is very vast. So vast that I am able to learn from intelligent, talented, beautiful people every day. The kind of people who have supported me and the team, the kind of people who are about realizing their dream. I am certain that together we are effecting the change we need. Our babies will not lack the necessary tools to advance their world. With the heart, understanding, and love of ten thousand ancestors, jere jef mboka!

Forward

Spear Masters: A Historical Survey of the Minds of African Warrior Scholars Vol.4

By sbA Mkuu Mzee

I am absolutely delighted to introduce to you the latest production in a long line of well-written and brilliantly conceived projects as appropriately titled above.

Each publication brings to the African Community different insights and elegant looks into the much-varied African tribal cultures and influences in and around the Mother Continent. I know that this latest collection Vol. 4, from the talented young Scholars of the Kofi Piesie Research Team in association with the Mossi Warrior Clan will bring many accurate revelations and dispel the purposeful disinformation and false narratives that have plagued us for so long by those who have written the narrative. It is our responsibility now to write our own narrative and lead our people down the path of scientific and factually researched literacy.

I find the choice of the title for the publications very interesting. Kofi Piesie and his team never construct any of their work by accident as it is truly designed to give the readers not only a sense of pride but to also incentivize them to investigate further the meaning and the impact of the moniker "Spears of the Mossi."

A quick overview reveals that the Mossi make up the largest ethnic group in Burkina Faso. They are the second-largest ethnic group in Côte d'Ivoire (Ivory Coast).

At one time, the Mossi were organized into three kingdoms, Tenkodogo, Wagadugu, and Yatenga. It is not clear when these were founded. However, a Mossi raid on the city of Timbuktu in 1329 is described in Arab history. Each Mossi village had its own chief, and groups of up to twenty villages were ruled by a district chief. The political system of the Mossi was very closely connected to their religion. For this reason, the Mossi rulers resisted conversion to Islam, even though other African groups accepted the new religion (after about the tenth century). The Mossi language is Moré.

It belongs to the Gur group within the Niger-Congo language family. Like many African languages, Moré uses pitch (how high or low a tone is) to distinguish meanings. Also, as in other African languages, a verb form shows whether its action is continuing or happens only once.

Other notable influences of the Spear in African societies can be found in the southern African spears, also known as assegais, which were the principal weapon of most groups/tribes there, except the Venda. Different types of spears were used for battles, hunting, and even fishing. Battle spears were the most popular as they were used for attack and defense. Most African tribes had spears that were made using a long wooden sheath and a metallic head as well as the bow and arrows and shields often made from animal hide. Some communities used what they called crafted swords.

The great Shaka of the Zulu invented a shorter stabbing spear with a two-foot (0.61m) shaft and a larger, broader blade one foot (0.3m) long. The traditional spear was not abandoned but was used to attack enemy formations before closing in for close-quarters battle with the iklwa. Furthermore, the Zulu, Xhosa, and other Nguni tribes of South Africa were renowned for their use of the assegai (spear).

All of these African groups were known for crafting unique weaponry during the pre-colonial era, which was then used for various activities like war, grazing, traditional ceremonies, and some even for prestige.

Iron smelting and forging technologies may have existed in West Africa among the Nok culture of Nigeria as early as the sixth century B.C. In the period from 1400 to 1600, iron technology appears to have been one of a series of fundamental social assets that facilitated the growth of significant centralized kingdoms in the western Sudan and along the Guinea coast of West Africa. The fabrication of iron tools and weapons allowed for the kind of extensive systematized agriculture, efficient hunting, and successful warfare necessary to sustain large urban centers.

Iron, like the tools and weapons forged from it, is highly valued in African societies across the continent. Among the

Chamba Daka speakers of the Shebsi Mountains, an iron spear with curliques and clappers was part of a chief's regalia and would be buried with him. In the masterful work "Spear Masters" by Dr. Molefi Asante found in the book "The Encyclopedia of African Religion," we find the mystical and spiritual importance of the spear in the Dinka society of the Sudan.

There is a generational oral story and tradition where the spear can indeed invoke new life where there was none before through the spirit world into the wife when the husband has suddenly transitioned. The concept of good and evil, just as in Maat, is prevalent in their spiritual life journey. In the end, the spear masters were those who followed the straight path, walked erect, and taught others the lessons of Aiwel that the spear could be used for good, as in fishing, or for defending the clan against enemies, as in warfare.

So, we see that the spear across the Mother Continent, especially before the onslaught of colonialism has always played an important part in the cultural identity of its' people. Without it, even now would strip many of our people across the African continental landscape of who we were, are, and how we developed our sense of community.

I am sure that you will enjoy this work by Kofi and my young brothers of the Kofi Piesie Research Team. I am proud and very comfortable to have these Africans take their place as the next intellectual movers and shakers of the community and am very honored to call them true Asafo (Warriors) and our Spear Masters.

Htp

Anx uja snb

Abibifahodie

Introduction

Introduction

Kofi Piesie

The title of this book, "Spear Masters," is inspired by the Dinka people of Southern Sudan. Before I get into the Dinka folktale about the Spear Masters, let's look at what a spear is and its origin.

Spear

A spear is a pole weapon consisting of a shaft, usually of wood, with a pointed head. The head may be simply the sharpened end of the shaft itself, as is the case with fire-hardened spears, or it may be made of a more durable material fastened to the shaft, such as bone, flint, obsidian, iron, steel, or bronze (or other types of stone or metal). Since ancient times, the most common design for hunting or combat spears has incorporated a metal spearhead shaped like a triangle, lozenge, or leaf. The heads of fishing spears usually feature barbs or serrated edges.

Origin

Archaeological evidence found in present-day Germany documents that wooden spears have been used for hunting since at least 400,000 years ago, and a 2012 study from the site of Kathu Pan in South Africa suggests that hominids, possibly Homo heidelbergensis, may have developed the technology of hafted stone-tipped spears in Africa about 500,000 years ago.

However, wood does not preserve well, and Craig Stanford, a primatologist and professor of anthropology at the University of Southern California, has suggested that the discovery of spear used by chimpanzees means that early humans may have used wooden spears before this.

I know you like huh chimpanzees use spears?

Chimpanzees are capable of making spears to hunt other primates and have been seen using the weapons to kill bushbabies for meat, scientists announced some time ago.

The scientists investigated the Fongoli community of savannah-dwelling chimpanzees(Pan troglodytes verus) in southeastern Senegal. The researchers saw ten different chimps fashioning spear-like tools to forcibly jab at nocturnal primates known as lesser bushbabies(Galago senegalensis), which sleep inside hollow branches or tree trunks during the day. After their attacks, the chimps sniffed or licked their weapons as if to see whether or not they shed blood.

In 2007 a group of researchers began a study of observing chimp behavior. During that time, they recorded 308 spear hunting events, which they noted, was more common for females than males; they accounted for 61 percent of the total. The researchers suggest this is likely the case because it is more difficult for females to chase down prey. After all, they almost always have offspring clinging to their bodies. To date, the chimps are the only known animal to use a tool as a weapon to hunt a "large" animal, other than humans—

chimps in other troops have been seen to use twigs as tools to help collect termites, but scientists do not count that as hunting.

"Spear Master"

According to the Dinka, the Spear Master are those who learned lessons of good and evil as represented in the use of the spear. We, the Kofi Piesie Research Team, are a group that has learned lessons of good and evil, as illustrated in the use of the pen. The pen, just like the spear, can be used for good or evil, but we use our pen/spear to fight against pseudoism, misinformation that might hurt and harm our people.

Now back to the Dinka, who says according to their folktale, that long ago, there were dances held by lions, and a man was dancing when a lion looked at him and demanded his bracelet. The man refused to give his bracelet to the lion, after which the lion bit his thumb entirely off. Then the man bled to death. The man had left a wife and daughter behind, but they had no son, and so the widow went weeping to the river. The river spirit heard her and asked her what was wrong. When she told the story of her misfortune, the river spirit said to her, "Lift your skirt and brush the waves toward you so that they enter your body."

The spirit gave her a spear and told her that the spear was a symbol of her bearing a male child. He also gave her a fish for food and told her to go home and relax without delay. The woman went home and soon bore a son, Aiwel, who had a complete set of teeth when he was born, a sign of unusual spiritual powers.

As an infant, he was left sleeping on the floor, but when the mother came back into the room, she noticed that a gourd of milk had been drunk. Not believing that it could have been the infant, she accused her daughter of stealing the milk. She punished the daughter. The same thing happened over and over again. The mother was quite disturbed by this situation and soon became suspicious. She acted like she was leaving the baby alone with the milk, but she thought she should hide herself in the bushes and watch the baby as she went out. She did this and, to her surprise, saw the baby Aiwel get up from the floor and drink the milk. She opened the door and accused him of drinking the milk. He told her not to tell anybody, or she would die. She could not keep the secret to herself, and she died as Aiwel had said. He had begun to develop the power of the Spear Masters to make his words come true.

He could no longer live with his family after his mother's death. He went to stay with the spirit father in the river until he grew up. He left the river as a man with an ox of many colors, representing all the colors of his cattle. The ox was named Longar, and from then on, the man was Aiwel Longar. Aiwel then decided to tell the village elders that they had to leave that place to avoid the death of all their cattle. He went and said to them that he would show them where there was a big pasture and no death. They refused to believe him. So, he went by himself and found the place, and his cattle prospered. But soon the people tried to follow him, but it was more difficult now. At one river where they were trying to cross, Aiwel stood on the other side of the river, encouraging them, but he would kill them with his spear as they came up out of the reeds.

Then one of the men, Agothyathik, saw what was happening and decided to play a trick on Aiwel. He would take a large ox bone and give it to a friend to take across the river, holding it on a pole in front of him as he crossed. When Aiwel saw this, he thought it was a human and tried to spear it. Just then, Agothyathik grabbed him and wrestled him to the ground. Finally, Aiwel tired and gave up the wrestling and told Agothyathik to bring the people over. Some were afraid, but to those who came, Aiwel gave fishing spears to carry when they prayed and war spears when they fought. He gave them deities to worship and a blue bull whose thighbone would be sacred to them. The men who received the spears became leaders of clans that are spear masters who keep the most perfect way. In the end, the Spear Masters were those who followed the straight path, walked erect, and taught others the lessons of Aiwel that the spear could be used for good, as in fishing, or for defending the clan against enemies as in warfare.

Aiwel Longar represents so many values, attitudes, and dispositions in Dinka philosophy that one could almost say that the Dinka measure other humans by the characteristics of Aiwel Longar. First of all, his narrative is epic and shows that he had arisen from a unique condition of being from the spiritual and the human side. Second, he overcame all conditions of difference and established himself as the leader of his people.

Part I (Dinka)

SURVEY ONE

The Dinka

Kofi Piesie

The Dinka are group into 20 tribes, and they live on the vast, flat savannah Sudan. They are the largest group in South Sudan, representing 35.8% and, depending on the source, between 1 and 4 million. The Dinka are one of the largest ethnic groups in Africa; they are also among the least touched by Western ways. Also, the Dinka, with other tribes in Sudan, formed the ancient Nubian kingdom. The Dinka, just like the other tribes such as Nuer, Turkana, Samburu, and Masai's, are some of the tallest people in the world. Males can have an average height of 1.9 m (6 ft, 4in), while women of 1.8 m (6 ft). These people have slim but strong bodies, and their heads are more elongated than in the typical African group.

Their world center on their cattle: The herdsmen must constantly move in search of pasture; their young men are learning the art of war to protect their cattle, and their girls are given in marriage in exchange for cattle. The Dinka worship a single all-powerful God, Nhialic, but he is a vague and shadowy being, and in everyday matters, it is the spirits, who are manifestations of Nhialic, that must be placated by offerings and sacrifices. Sacrifice marks every stage of Dinka's life-birth, initiation, marriage, parenthood, death, and each movement in the early cycle of the tribes. (Ryle, John. Warrior of the White Nile. Time-Life Books, 1982.)

The Dinka are one of the branches of the River Lake Nilotes. Though known for centuries as Dinka, they call themselves Jieng (Upper Nile) or Muonyjang ("people of the people" or "men among men," for the Dinka see themselves as the standard against which all other men must be judged.

On the first page of this chapter, I mention that Dinka are split up into 20 or more tribes, each of which is further divided into several tribes' groups that occupy a geographical area that is large enough to provide sufficient water and pasture for their herds of cattle. Each subtribe has its own elected chief, but these chiefs wield influence rather than power, and the Dinka has no overall structure of authority. Let's look at the folktale or cosmology story of the Dinka to see why Dinka basically governor their selves and chief wield their influence rather than power.

Dinka Folktale

The Dinka's first ancestors, Mayual, came from the sky. He took a Dinka girl for his wife, and she conceived. But, before the child was born, Mayual returned to the sky. Then digging holes in the ground, he built his byre by planting the short people as uprights and using the tall people as rafters, lashing them to the central supports. Every eight years, he replaced them with other human victims. When Cikom's son Ding came of age, the people of the camp visited Ding secretly and asked: Is this a good thing that your father does, this planting of people? Soon there will be too few of us left to defend the cattle. Their arguments persuaded Ding, and so that very day, after the herds had been released for grazing, he dug a deep pit in the dry earth and called his father. When his father Cikom came, Ding pushed him into the hole and cried out to the men of the camp to hold him down. A bull was sacrificed on top of the struggling man, and the grave was covered with earth mud.

This strange and violent legend of a chief who grew too powerful and came tyrannized his subjects reflects the Dinka's profound wariness of all established authority. At the same time, it implicitly underscores their emphasis on leadership: to overthrow Cikom, the men of the camp had first to persuade his son Ding to accept responsibility for himself. Such myths also express the sense the Dinka have of a violent past, a time punctuated with civil discord and natural disasters when, as they say, "There was no law." In the sequel to this tale, Ding himself becomes a tyrant and takes to spearing men in the river as if they were as many fish until he is overthrown.

Traditionally, however, Dinka chiefs have exercised authority by persuasion, not by force: they have no power to command other members of the tribes. To outsiders, indeed, it has often seemed that the Dinka are people without rulers. There are chiefs in each tribal section, but few have authority over a whole tribe. There are chiefs of each camp, strong men whose main role is to keep the peace, but they have power only in their own camps. The most influential men are the spiritual leaders, the Chiefs of the Fishing Spears -so-called because spears are the symbols of their office, who among the Agar have generally refused to accept secular authority. (Ryle, John. Warrior of the White Nile. Time-Life Books, 1982.)

Dink Initiation

Initiation marks a young man's passage from boyhood to adulthood. An initiate is called a parapool - "one who has stopped milking." Initiation means he no longer does a boy's work of milking, tethering the cattle, and carting dung. So, for some of the younger boys, the harvest marks a more solemn occasion: this is the time of year when adolescents are initiated into manhood and become parapuol. Each boy's head will be cut in six horizontal lines that mark him for life as a Dinka and declare him eligible for marriage. The horizontal lines carve in the young man's forehead do more than identify tribal loyalties; they also show that the wearer has been initiated into manhood and no longer does a boy's work of milking and carting dung. The initiations take place at the ages of 10 to 16.

The six lines on the young man's forehead also declare him to be a warrior and seen to be brave. If one of the young men flinch during the operation, the kink resulting from the path of the knife will mark him as a coward for the rest of his life. The scarring ceremony takes place before the second durra crop was harvested, and before the event, there is singing and dancing for several days. The night before initiation, the boys will be taken to a house where they will sit together and sing the songs of their clans. Somebody would come to the house and shaved young boy's heads, and all were steadfast and ready. At the first sign of dawn, their parents will arrive and led them rapidly to another homestead where the initiator was waiting. The parents of the young boys would take a yellow cucumber, which symbolizes health and well-being. Their parents would then wave the yellow cucumber above the bare head. The initiator will lead the young boys into a field in line with their backs facing the rising sun. (Fisher, Angela, and Carol Beckwith. Dinka: Legendary Cattle Keepers of Sudan. Rizzoli, 2010.)

The parents and relatives would watch them each dig a hole between his thighs to catch the blood. After the holes are dung, the initiator would stand before the young boy and hold the crown of their head steady with his hand. Each young boy would always look straight in front of him into the distance and be relaxed. The initiator would grip the blade, and one by one, he would slice a line right across the boy's forehead, starting above one ear and turning the boy's head to complete the cut in a single motion. In a loud and clear voice, the boys would call out the names of their ancestors as his family and the other boys look on, betraying no emotions.

When all initiates have been ritually scarred, their fathers wipe the blood from their sons' eyes and mouths, then wrap a broad leaf around their foreheads. Initiation scars mean that a man is able to marry - the parapuol may now begin to court eligible girls. The boys are presented with a spear, a club, and a shield - necessary accouterments of a warrior.

There is great rejoicing within the group, with singing and dancing going on for several days. After his initiation, a parapuol is given an ox, his "song oxen." It is his most precious possession, and he will lavish care on it, even to the extent of delicately. (Fisher, Angela, and Carol Beckwith. Dinka: Legendary Cattle Keepers of Sudan. Rizzoli, 2010.)

Today, most Dinka-educated Dinka are opposed to scaring, and the government has even tried to ban it. Still, to the Dinka of the villages and camps, it continues to be a mark of honoring and proofing manhood. Boys sent away to school, who would not usually be initiate, sometimes go back voluntarily.

Ox For the Young Men

The ox is giving to every Dinka youth soon after his initiation into manhood. The ox becomes his most precious possession; he spares no pains to cultivate its appearance and never tires of composing the songs he constantly sings in its honor. To distinguish his young "song ox" from all others, a Dinka will have its horns trained to be special-shaped by having them cut so that the outgrowths will curve in new directions. This delicate task is usually left to a horn designer of proven skill. He first softens each horn by exposing it to the heat of a smoldering log, then cuts across it diagonally with a newly sharpened spearhead. The horns are tied at the base with bark fibre to stem the blood that will ooze from the marrow when they are shaved at the angle determined by the designer. As the horns grow, they will curve in the direction of the angled, exposed surface.

The origins of the custom are not known, but it may have been practiced long ago by the ancient Egyptians. Some 1,500 miles to the north, in the tomb of Menufer, who lived in the third millennium B.C., there is an illustration of a bull with one horn curving down almost into its eyes, an exaggerated form of the deliberate deformation that is practiced among the Dinka to this day. During the lifetime of a song ox, its owner may perform two or three such impromptu sacrifices, perhaps on the occasion of its castration at the age of eight or nine months. A few months later, when the young calf by then a yearling has its horns cut so that, as they grow, they will curve in opposite directions, one forwards and one backward.

The song ox must undergo one final alteration. The nerveless tips of the horns, when fully grown, are pierced with the narrow point of a red-hot fishing spear. From each horn, the owner will then suspend a black tassel made of hair from a buffalo's tail or, failing that, of a cow. Between a young man and his song ox, there exists a very close relationship. Should the animal die or be taken away as part of a marriage agreement, its owner feels grief and pain over the loss until he can transfer his affection to another animal. No one is ever ashamed of his ox; if its color is undistinguished, an owner will eulogize its spreading horns, the skill with which it flicks its lowing with his own song. His ox is, by definition, perfect.

Men And Women Corset (Malual)

The Dinka wear few clothes, particularly in their own village. Adult men wear a corset known as "malual.' It exposes many parts of their body except for beads around the neck or wrist. "The tight beaded corsets indicate the men's position in the age-set system of the tribe. The corsets are first sewn in place at puberty and not removed until the wearer reaches a new age set. Each group wears a color-coded corset: a red and blue corset indicates a man between fifteen and twenty-five years of age; a yellow and blue one marks someone over thirty and ready for marriage." (Dink People: The Great Cattle Herders of Sudan, Blogger, 5 Nov. 2013, kwekudee-tripdownmemorylane.blogspot.com/2012/10/dinka-people-great-cattle-herders-of.html0.)

The women commonly wear only goatskin skirts, but unmarried adolescent girls will typically be nude. These garments are used to communicate characteristics such as gender, age, wealth, and ethnic affiliation. (Dink People: The Great Cattle Herders of Sudan, Blogger, 5 Nov. 2013, kwekudee-tripdownmemorylane.blogspot.com/2012/10/dinka-people-great-cattle-herders-of.html.)

The women also wore a corset vest, and the male corset is easily recognized by its "horn" (fungi), flinging itself toward the sky at the back of the body. The rigid vertical strip that runs down the back represents his wealth. Here, it rises well above the shoulders, indicating to other Dinka people that the man's family had quite a large herd. The female corset vest has cowrie shells sewn at the front and back of the female vest to protect the wearer and ensure her fertility. Both corset and vest come in different colors, each linked to a particular age group. A man in his early twenties would have worn the corset, and a married woman in her late twenties the vest."

Body Decorations

The Dinka use their bodies as canvases which create living art. Young people especially may spend hours each day looking at nature as a tool to help them express themselves artistically by decorating and using their skin and hair as an artistic expression that defines the meaning of who they are.

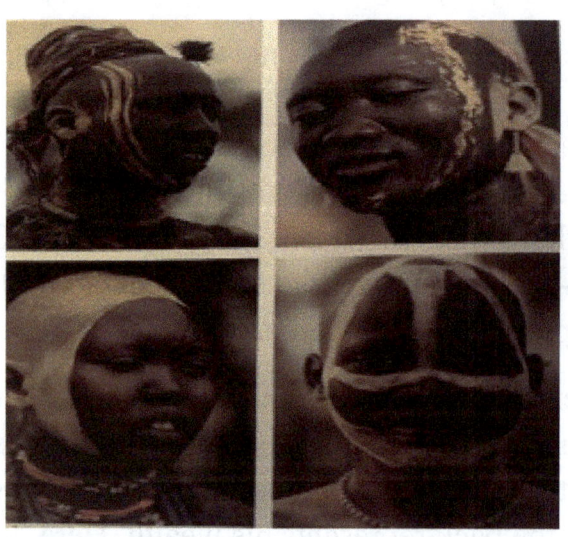

First, they anoint their bodies entirely with oil made from milk or prepared from the fruit of the shea butter tree; then, they apply an ash paste arranged in bold patterns that stand out vividly on their gleaming skin. The designs they affect are mostly a matter of personal whim, and fashions change every few years. Like many ethnic groups in Sudan, body paint is classified as an essential tribal activity, and since mirrors are rare, mutual grooming is usual. Friends with great care shave and trim each other's hair into neat shapes, and the finished styles may be set off with a brightly colored scarf on an elegant plume of ostrich feathers.

Marriages and Bride Price

Marriage is obligatory among the Dinka. Polygamy is allowed among the Dinka, though many men may have only one wife. The Dinka must marry outside their clan (exogamy), which promotes more cohesion across the broader Dinka group. Once a man has met a girl he wants to marry and established that she belongs to a different clan, thereby avoiding the risk of incest, he must consult his family to secure their approval. If they encourage him, his next step is to call on the girl's family to show that his interest is serious. He must impress them with a respectful demeanor and show that his family, too, is worthy of respect. To accomplish his aim, he will usually take two or three friends with him to support his suit and may even take two or three friends with him to support his suit and may even take his favorite ox as well. (Fisher, Angela, and Carol

Beckwith. Dinka: Legendary Cattle Keepers of Sudan. Rizzoli, 2010.)

Young Dinka men would parade their ox around their girlfriend hearth, accompanied by friends, while young Dinka led the animal, a magnificent beast with a deep chest and high curving hump. The bell hung around the ox neck clung at every step, as the ox owner would sing, extolling the virtue of the girl they are dating. Once the young men have been accepted as suitors, a man will make frequent visits to his girl and often stay the night with her; spinning tales' hour after hour, delighting the girl with protestation of love and boast of manliness and assurance of wealth.

A girl from a good family is likely to have several suitors, but she will typically follow the wishes of her relatives in choosing among them. A man from a poor family applying to one that is richer may be quickly discouraged and simply turned away to find sooner or later a humbler family to whom his modest bride price looks desirable. The girl's family will probably prefer a man from the same village or camp or a man from farther away, because it is easier for them to preserve their affectionate ties with their daughter and because it links two clans of the same settlement, reinforcing the loyalties and stability of the local community.

Even when both families look with favor on a possible match, a suitor may take months to prod his relatives into generosity in contributing cattle. The young men would compose songs deprecating their meanness or praising their open-handedness and sing them in public so that everyone may hear. But until the bride wealth is sufficient to satisfy the girl's kin, marriage is out of the question. Then, at the climax of the long procedure, when the two families meet to complete their negotiations, the suitor will virtually be ignored; and the elders of the families will take over. The negotiations can take up to hours, and bride price can be up to 60 cattle. If the families can't come to a mutual agreement, then there will be no marriage. There even suggested that paternal uncle would have to provide one of his best cattle to the family. Sometimes there are two suitors, and the family picks the best suitor to be married to their daughter, meaning the one who offers the more cattle.

Love of the Cattle

The Dinka lifestyle centered on their cattle, and the Dinka love their cattle. The Dinka themselves feel they are not so much in control of the cattle they own as subject to them. A traditional Dinka story makes their attitude clear. Long ago, the legend says the first warriors went hunting and killed the mother of both the first buffalo and the first cow. The animals vowed to take vengeance on their oppressor, but they chose to fight back in different ways. The buffalo decided to roam the forest and plain and attack man whenever he saw him. The cow was more subtle. She allowed herself to be caught and domesticated, then eventually made man dependent on her. Thus, Dinka became obliged to supply her needs and even die for her.

The Dinka would indeed lay down their lives to protect their animals, and sometimes they have to. The cattle are vital to Dinka's livelihood. Although they do not slaughter animals regularly for meat, the Dinka put their herds to almost every other use to supply their material needs. In the wet season, fresh milk is an essential part of every person's diet. The women churn some of the milk into butter by swirling it around inside a gourd. The butter is then usually boiled to transform into an oil used to cook and rub on the skin as body decoration. Besides providing a liquid for washing and dyeing hair, Cattle urine is also used for tanning hides. The unfailing supply of dung fuels the constantly smoldering fires, and the resulting ash is put to a range of uses, both practical and aesthetic: mixed with water, it makes a paste for cleaning teeth; rubbed on to the skin, it is decorative and, some Dinka claims, helps repel insects. (Asante , Molefi Kente, and Ama Mazama . Encyclopedia of African Religion. SAGE, 2009.) Whenever an animal dies, whether from old age or an accident, or by sacrifice, nothing is wasted. The meat is eaten, and the hide is cured for sleeping mats, drums, skins, ropes, halters, and belts.

But the practical uses of cattle are only a small part of their true value and significance to their owners. In a community that traditionally has had no overall ruler or central government, cattle are dispensable to the smooth-running Dinka society. Constantly changing hands, they are the medium through which important relationships are expressed, and their circulation maps the lines of Dinka loyalties and obligations. Dinka will give up their cattle voluntarily only in exchange for other cattle, to seal a family alliance, or as a religious offering in the form of a sacrifice. Bride wealth, the payment of cattle that seals a marriage, is contributed by the groom's relative in proportion among the bride's relatives, thus binding two families many times over.

Cattle may also be given in compensation for civil offenses, such as the elopement, for killings; a man found guilty of manslaughter might be ordered by the courts' chief to pay 30 cows to his victim's family. Murders are also tried in the government courts and may be sentences to prison terms of execution. The Dinka measure wealth chiefly in terms of cattle, and cattle plays an essential part in maintaining the broadly egalitarian nature of their society. Since wealth is in the form of cattle; cattle are always susceptible to the vagaries of climate and disease, and the demands of family may swell the family herd greatly by attracting bride wealth from families at each marriage, but a few sons will deplete the herd again when they, too, marry. The more cattle a man has, the more cattle a man has, the more relatives will turn to him for bride wealth contribution, and the larger his contribution will be.

The qualities of the Dinka value most in a man are those that make him a good herdsman.

1. Courage

2. Endurance

3. Stoicism

4. Self-Sufficiency

Spears are the badge of the herdsman. The older Dinka, stressing the central features of their life, says: "God gave the white man the gun and the pen, but to us, he gave us the spear and the cow."

We talk about the cows are the center of the Dinka life as well as the spear. The parapuol carries several light, flat-bladed spears balanced over one shoulder so that they can throw two or three times before retrieving his weapons. Dinka youth can, with ease and great accuracy, hurl a spear some 50 yards, launching it from the hip with arm outstretched and whole body arching backward for the throw. The Dinka has a disdain for weapons like bow and arrows, traps when they hunt cats, gazelles, elephants, and buffalo. We should all know their choice of weapons by now, and that's the spear

The rhythm of Dinka life is ordered by two sharply contrasting seasons: a period of total dryness lasting from November until April, followed by six months of rains. As each climatic turnabout transforms the landscape, families move to a land that can best support them and their cattle.

In the heat of the dry season, well in some of the woodland village, dry up, and the grass on the open plains' withers and browns. Before these sites become too inhospitable, the Dinka deserts them and heads toward the rivers, gradually shrinking to muddy pools. Near the riverbanks, the Dinka pasture their cattle and grow tobacco. In late March or April, a spate of heavy showers ends the long, dry winter. Pools in the riverbeds fill to overflowing, and a flush of tender grass spreads quickly over the plain. As the downpours continue, the rivers swell and eventually burst their banks. Within weeks the low pasture is inundated, and the Dinka retreat to higher ground. Families split up: some members move to wet season cattle camps on the newly watered grasslands away from the rivers, while others return to the homesteads in the woodlands to sow cereal crops in the well-drained sandy soil. By November, when all the crops are harvested, the receding floods again draw the Dinka riverwards. (Ryle, John. Warrior of the White Nile. Time-Life Books, 1982.)

Fishing Festival

At the beginning of April each year, thousands of Dinka from dozens of camps gather in a festive mood to spend several days fishing in a stretch of the River Naam and Lake Akeu nearby. One of the tribe's big annual occasions, the communal fishing, takes place at the end of the long dry season when the fish spawned in large numbers in the wet season floodwaters a few months previously have retreated to the last remaining pools. The gathered clans make the most of the resulting feast and reunion with friends and relatives from the scattered camps.

After a long wait, while the crowd gossip and sing, a small group of elders chants a prayer gesture rhythmically with their sticks and spears before sacrificing the hen to ensure a successful fishing festival. "Spear, do not pierce our feet, but only the fish," chants one of them. "Fish, come out to be eaten." And finally, "hen, I make an offering of you. "As soon as the hen has been drowned, the tribesmen plunge into the water, using spears and nets to land the fish and then passing over the catch to their families who wait on the bank. They cook most of the fish daily to eat on the spot;

any leftovers are filleted and hung to dry in the sun and later sold in the market. (Ryle, John. Warrior of the White Nile. Time-Life Books, 1982.) Also, when crops are about to be sown at the start of each rainy season, the Dinka offer a bull in sacrifice to their God Nhialic. The animal's life is given as a benediction for the new plantings and to ensure the prosperity and well-being of the community during the ensuing year. The ritual slaying ends a two-day seeding blessing ceremony held each year at the same shrine.

During the sacrifice of the bull, the religious leader would assemble his relatives around the bull, which one of them would provide, and each man, in turn, recited a litany chanting a list of requests that the doomed animal was to carry to God. The tribesmen also asserted their worthiness to receive such divine blessing by singing battle songs that celebrate their bravery and prowess as warriors and their victories in past conflicts. Before the bull was finally slain, they showed it the respect due to an intermediary with God, even sharpening the animal's horns to helps it vanquish hostile spirits that might try to bar its passage. When the chanting and singing reach a climax, the celebrants fell upon the bull, throwing it to the ground before the religious leader slits the bull's throat with the tip of the spear.

Just like I spoke about in the introduction, the title of this book is inspired by the Dinka People. I hope this first chapter gave you, the reader, a great insight into who this warrior type, spear toating, and cattle-loving people are. Modernity and foreign ideas have permeated Dinka culture and are slowly replacing their traditions and customs. They have adopted either jellabia or European dress, and now nudity and wearing of skins are rare even in the cattle camps. In the Next chapter, I will discuss how the Dinka slowly begin to lose their customs due to invaders such as the Arab and European and long-lasting wars.

SURVEY TWO

Lost Boys of Sudan

Kofi Piesie

Before I discuss the lost boys of Sudan, I want to discuss the Anglo-Egyptian combined government, their motives of conquest in Sudan, and the first and second civil wars, leading up to Sudan's lost boys. In the 1890s, British forces invaded the Mahdi's Sudan, bringing it under their control, imposing their policies, and filling the top administrative posts with British officials. Now, as a result of the growing economic, political, and social corruption in the reign of Mahdi caliphs under the succession of Muhammad Ahmad al-Mahdi, in 1898, Anglo-Egyptian combined forces through advanced weaponry, military tactics, and training were able to gain complete control of the Sudan following the battle of Omdurman capturing the capital city of Khartoum under the leadership of Herbert Kitchener. Following this initial conquest of the Sudan and removal of the Mahdists, the Anglo-Egyptian forces were able to fully establish their existence and influence within the colony of Sudan through the action of several treaties and administrative policies establishing the Anglo-Egyptian combined condominium power with the Sudan under the leadership of both the British Crown and the Egyptian Khedive. As stated in Lord Cromer's Memorandum regarding the functions of the condominium, "the Khedive is under an obligation to follow English advice in all important matters," which truly establishes the British dominance and control in this imperial relationship. In turn, this furthered the age of political instability and leadership rotation throughout the history of the Sudanese administration.

Egyptian Motives for Conquest

Although there was an Anglo-Egyptian combined government administration and military system following the conquest of the Mahdi Sudan, Egypt and Great Britain as individual governments and nations had different motivations of conquering the Sudan and colonizing it. Under the colonial rule of Britain at the time, the Egyptians sought to establish both a sense of national power, superiority, and liberty while under Britain's control. Through conquering Sudan alongside the British, Egypt gained a sense of superiority and control over the people of another nation, allowing for them to establish a sense of national authority and power while still controlled by the British. The main goal for the national Egyptian powers was to maintain the stability of their economic trading systems, in which gaining control over the Sudan allowed for their continual accessibility to trade markets, resources, and trade routes along the White and Blue Nile. Under the corrupt Mahdi rule, Egyptian economic trading practices along the Nile in Sudan were strained and heavily deteriorated due to the lack of accessibility to resources and markets in the Sudan. Furthermore, Egypt's combined conquest of Sudan allowed for Egypt to re-establish its economic prosperity in terms of gaining profit, increasing activity, and product demand in the economy as a result of control over the Sudanese Nile.

British Motives for Conquest of the Sudan

Like the Egyptians, the British sought to gain control over the Sudan to establish both a settler and plantation-based colony that would allow them to gain more accessibility to the Nile, trade routes, and trading markets. This access to the Nile and its trade markets allowed the British to gain significant amounts of profit from the sale and trading of British manufactured goods, including textiles, alcohol, and guns, and establishing new trading relationships with the growing cities. Along with this, the British heavily desired to gain access to the existing natural resources in Sudan with a specific interest in the cotton supply. Cotton would prove to be beneficial in further providing cotton to the manufacturing companies in the capitalist textile industry. This influx of cotton allowed the textile industry to produce a surplus of textiles that allowed the industry and Great Britain to gain more wealth and profits from the constant supply and demand for textiles. As a result of the growth of nationalist competition throughout Europe, the British sought to establish a sense of nationalist power and international dominance by gaining yet another rich African territory like Sudan. This addition of the Sudan gave Great Britain further authoritative leverage on its European competitors with the purpose of achieving global dominance.

Second Sudanese Civil War (1955 -1972)

The First Sudanese Civil War was a seventeen-year conflict between Sudan's northern and southern regions between 1955 and 1972. The war began a year before Sudan was declared independent from Great Britain. The main belligerents in the war were the central government of Sudan and the Southern Sudan Liberation Movement (SSLM). Great Britain, Egypt, and the Soviet Union supported the central government, while Ethiopia, Uganda, and Israel backed the SSLM. An estimated 500,000 people died during the seventeen-year conflict. (Momodu, S. (2020, January 22). First Sudanese Civil War (1955-1972). BlackPast.org. https://www.blackpast.org/global-african-history/events-global-african-history/first-sudanese-civil-war-1955-1972/)

The root of the conflict can be traced to when the British governed Sudan as a colony; they administered the northern and southern provinces separately. The South was more like the other East-African colonies – Kenya, Tanzania, and Uganda – while northern Sudan was more identical to Arabic-speaking Egypt. Northern Arabs were prevented from holding positions of power in the South with its African traditions, and trade was discouraged between the two areas. However, in 1946, the British gave in to northern pressure to integrate the two areas. Arabic was made the language of administration in the South, and northerners began to hold positions there. The southern elite, trained in English, resented the change as they were kept out of their own government. After decolonization, most powers were given to the northern elites based in Khartoum, causing unrest in the South.

In 1953 the British moved towards granting Sudan independence, but they failed to give enough power to Southern leaders. Southern Sudanese leaders weren't even invited to negotiations during the transitional period in the 1950s. In the post-colonial government of 1953, the Sudanization Committee only included six southern leaders, though there were some 800 available senior administrative positions. (Karl R. DeRouen and Uk Heo. Civil wars of the world: major conflicts since World War II.) On August 18, 1955, the Equatoria Corps, composed mainly of British Colonial soldiers from southern Sudan, attempted to disperse a crowd of protesters in Torit, Sudan (now Torit, South Sudan). However, the southern soldiers appeared to be sympathetic to the protesters, prompting the central government in Khartoum (the capital of Sudan) to replace them with troops from the northern region. Outraged, the southern soldiers mutinied, killing 336 northerners, both soldiers and civilians. News of the Torit mutiny spread, and southern soldiers across Sudan revolted. Other factors influenced the conflict as well. The Northern two-thirds of Sudan were overwhelmingly Muslim, while Christianity or indigenous religions were most popular in the South. Culturally, Northern Sudanese people spoke Arabic and identified with Saudi Arabia and North Africa, while the Southerners looked to Ethiopia and the newly independent states of Sub-Saharan Africa.

Since Southern Sudanese forces lacked the infrastructure to launch a major offensive against the north, they launched a guerrilla war. They were also the first insurgency to recruit child soldiers. As the fighting progressed, Southern Sudanese rebels divided into two factions. One group, the Sudan African National Union (SANU), was formed and led by William Deng from the Dinka ethnic group. Another faction, the Anya Nya, was founded and led by Joseph Lagu and was composed mostly of the Madi group. The war created problems for the government in Khartoum as well. Because Northern forces were unable to put down the rebellion, several coups brought about new governments. In 1965, ten years after the civil war began, interim prime minister Muhammad Ahmad Mahgoub offered amnesty to the Southern Sudanese rebels if they would lay down their arms. The rebels rejected the offer, and the fighting continued.

By 1970 the civil war had taken about 500,000 lives, mainly in the South. In 1969, General Gaafar Nimeri took control of the Sudanese government and instituted a socialist program that included nationalizing banks and other businesses. He received crucial military support from the Soviet Union. Two years later, after attempted assassination by Sudanese communists, Nimeri, on July 19, 1971, renounced socialism and invited foreign investors into Sudan. Eight months later, on March 27, 1972, the government in Khartoum and the Southern rebels signed the Addis Ababa Agreement, which ended the First Sudanese Civil War. The country of Sudan remained in an uneasy peace for eleven years until a much larger and bloodier conflict called the Second Sudanese Civil War began in 1983. (Momodu, S. (2020, January 22). First Sudanese Civil War (1955-1972). BlackPast.org. https://www.blackpast.org/global-african-history/events-global-african-history/first-sudanese-civil-war-1955-1972/)

The Addis Ababa Accords

According to the Addis Ababa Agreement, the entire South would comprise one region with its own assembly and elected executive. The region had an independent budget and tax source to control internal security and local administration in the social, cultural, and education fields. English, rather than Arabic, was recognized as the principal language in the South. Moreover, the Addis Ababa agreement specified that the guerrilla forces, known as Anya Nya, would be gradually absorbed into the army and would serve in the South; Thereby relinquishing their demand for independence to gain substantial self-rule and protection from pressure from the center. (Wama, Barnabas L. Prolonged Wars: The War in Sudan. Biblioscholar, 2012.)

Second Sudanese Civil War (1983-2005)

The Second Sudanese Civil War was an intense 22-year conflict between the central government in Khartoum and the Sudan People's Liberation Army (SPLA). The war started in southern Sudan but spread to other places, including the Nuba Mountains and the Blue Nile region. Two million people died in this conflict, but the war also led to the creation of South Sudan as an independent nation in 2011. The terms of the Addis Ababa Agreement in 1972, which ended the first Sudan Civil War, were violated several times. In 1978, president Gaafar Nimeiry wanted to take control of the newly discovered oil fields located on the border region between north and South Sudan. In 1983, President Nimeiry violated the agreement by imposing Sharia Law across the nation and abolishing the predominantly Christian Southern Sudan Autonomous Region. Sharia Law now punished most South Sudanese people and other people who were non-Muslim living in the north. (Momodu, S. (2018, December 23). Second Sudanese Civil War (1983-2005). BlackPast.org. https://www.blackpast.org/global-african-history/events-global-african-history/second-sudanese-civil-war-1983-2005/)

As stated, President Nimeiri in 1983 imposed Shari'a law, resulting in the death of a million in half Sudanese. In response, the Sudan People's Liberation Movement (SPLM) started, a body created by the Sudan People's Liberation Army (SPLA).

SPLA(Sudan People's Liberation Army)

The SPLA was formed in 1983 when Lieutenant Colonel John Garang of the SPAF was sent to quell a mutiny in Bor of 500 southern troops who were resisting orders to be relocated to the north. Instead of ending the mutiny, Garang encouraged mutinies in other garrisons and set himself at the head of the rebellion against the Khartoum government.

Garang, a Dinka born into a Christian family, had studied at Grinnell College, Iowa, and later returned to the United States to take a company commanders' course at Fort Benning, Georgia, and again to earn advanced economics degrees at Iowa State University. By 1986 the SPLA was estimated to have 12,500 adherents organized into twelve battalions and equipped with small arms and a few mortars. By 1989 the SPLA's strength had reached 20,000 to 30,000; by 1991, it was estimated at 50,000 to 60,000.

Since 1983, the SPLA has been divided into three main factions: the SPLA Torit faction led by John Garang; the SPLA Bahr-al-Ghazal faction led by Carabino Kuany Bol; and the South Sudan Independence Movement led by Rick Machar. These internal divisions have intensified fighting in the South, hampering any potential peace settlement. The SPLA remains the principal military force in the insurgency. About 34 years ago, Sudan's civil war uprooted 20,000 Nuer and Dinka. They were known as the Lost Boys. According to the International Rescue Committee, in 1987, the civil war drove an estimated 20,000 young boys from their families and villages in southern Sudan. Most just six or seven years old, they fled to Ethiopia to escape death or induction into the northern army. They walked more than a thousand miles, half of them dying before reaching Kakuma refugee camp in Kenya. The survivors of this tragic exodus became known as the Lost Boys of Sudan.

During the Second Sudanese Civil War, Emmanuel Jal states that children could not support themselves adequately and suffered greatly from the terror. Many children were orphaned or separated from their families because of the systematic attacks of genocide in the southern part of the country. Some children were able to avoid capture or death because they were away from their villages tending cattle at the cattle camps (grazing land located near bodies of water where cattle were taken and tended largely by the village children during the dry season) and were able to flee and hide in the dense African bush. Some of the unaccompanied male minors were conscripted by the Islamic Southern rebel terrorist forces and used as soldiers in the rebel army, while others were handed over to the Islamic State by their own families to ensure protection, for food, and under a false impression, the child would be attending school. Children were highly marginalized during this period. As a result, they began to conglomerate and organize themselves to flee the country and the war.

The previous paragraph is a first-hand account Emmanuel Jal saw and experience as a young boy in Sudan. Emmanuel Jal was born in war-ravaged Sudan; Emmanuel Jal was kidnapped from his home and taken to fight alongside the army made up of rebels in the civil war. He does not remember how old he was when he was taken, nor did he know the exact year he was born. He speculates that he was six or seven years when he was taken. Emmanuel was a 'warrior child' that fought with an AK-47 rifle that was much larger than he could carry at the time for five years and managed to survive in the mass human graveyards. When he was thirteen years old, he already had been part of two civil wars and had witnessed other children's soldiers being abused. After suffering through much trauma, he was smuggled to Kenya, to the city of Nairobi by a British aid worker. After gaining international recognition, tv channels like MTV and CNN have broadcasted his message of peace all around the world.

A documentary about his life won the prestigious award 'Cadilac Audience' at the Tribeca Film Festival in New York. St. Martin press published Emmanuel Jal's book, an autobiography, in 2009. Although he has not forgotten about his native Sudan, Emmanuel now divides his time between London and Nairobi. He is the founder of a non-profit organization called Gua Africa, which aims to provide education to young children that have been affected by war and are impoverished by it in the region of Sub-Saharan Africa. He one day hopes to build a school in South Sudan, in his hometown of Leer, that even until the present day sees the largest number of child soldiers in the region. The 20,000 Sudanese children fled their homeland in search of safety in what turned out to be a treacherous 1,000-mile journey to Ethiopia. Wandering in and out of war zones, these "Lost Boys" spent the next four years in dire conditions. Thousands of boys lost their lives to hunger, dehydration, and exhaustion. Some were attacked and killed by wild animals; others drowned crossing rivers, and many were caught in the crossfire of fighting forces.

Kakuma refugee camp

In 1991, the war in Ethiopia sent the young refugees fleeing again, and approximately a year later, they began trickling into northern Kenya. Some 10,000 boys, between the ages of eight and 18, eventually made it to the Kakuma refugee camp—a sprawling, parched settlement of mud huts where they would live for the next eight years under the care of refugee relief organizations like the IRC. The IRC began working in Kakuma in 1992 to assist the Lost Boys and other refugees fleeing the fighting in Sudan. Its programs expanded over time to include all of the camp's health services treating refugees who arrived malnourished or sick, offering rehabilitation programs for those who were disabled, and working to prevent outbreaks of disease.

Older boys took part in IRC education programs and received support to learn trades and start small businesses to earn money to supplement relief rations. The IRC also helped these young entrepreneurs start savings accounts and access small loans to invest in their futures. "The IRC's health, sanitation, community services, and education programs touched, in one way or another, the lives of all the Lost Boys who were in Kakuma and who were eventually resettled in the U.S.A.," recalled Jason Phillips, who managed IRC programs in the camp from 2000 to 2001. "We accompanied and supported them throughout a large part of their journey."

A refuge in the United States

As the war in Sudan continued to rage, the United Nations refugee agency (UNHCR) determined that repatriation and family reunification was no longer an option for the Lost Boys. UNHCR recommended approximately 3,600 of them for resettlement in the United States, and the U.S. State Department concurred. The Kakuma youth began arriving in the U.S. in small groups in the fall of 2000. Over the next year, the IRC helped hundreds resettle in and around Atlanta, Boston, Dallas, Phoenix, Salt Lake City, San Diego, Seattle, and Tucson. Because many of the newly arrived Lost Boys were over 18 and considered adults, they were not placed into foster care. "We place the older boys together in apartments to try to maintain the kind of support network that they developed throughout their difficult journey and while living in the Kakuma camp," said Jon Merrill, who was then director of the IRC's resettlement program in Tucson. "They have been like family to each other for so long now, so it's best for them to continue to live as a family unit here."

Quest for education

Most of the older boys who came to the United States were eager to capitalize on opportunities for higher education but found that their idea of becoming full-time students was not a realistic goal. Since most were over 18 and living on their own, they needed to support themselves. And even though the majority attended school within Kakuma camp and had completed or were well on their way to completing high school, they did not necessarily qualify for entry into U.S. colleges. For these young men, IRC staff members stressed the importance of finding a job soon after arrival and continuing their educational pursuits part-time. The IRC helped the Lost Boys find jobs with local employers and connected them with volunteer mentors for help studying for exams to enable them to receive a General Equivalency Diploma (GED), and in turn, apply for college.

Adjusting to life in America

The Lost Boys faced enormous challenges in adjusting to American culture and modern society. IRC caseworkers worked closely with the boys in orienting them to their new communities, making sure that they were as comfortable as possible, and offering guidance on such issues as personal safety, social customs, public transportation, shopping, cooking, nutrition, and hygiene. Volunteers, many of whom became aware of the immense needs of this group through media coverage, also played a significant role in this area. They served as an essential link to the greater community, helping to generate additional employment opportunities, as well as increase donations and awareness. Volunteers at the IRC's Boston office (now closed) took part in a mentoring program for newly arrived Kakuma youth, providing support and guidance, and organizing recreational activities to bring the young men together. Many of the Lost Boys resettled by the IRC also took part in IRC programs aimed at helping them cope with their traumatic past and easing their transition into such a different culture. The IRC's Phoenix resettlement office, for example, worked with clinical psychologists to provide specialized counseling services.

Over the next decade, the Lost Boys built new lives for themselves in their adopted country. Many of them went on to earn college degrees and attain U.S. citizenship while wondering whether they someday could return to their homeland and reunite with the families they left behind. Then, in 2005, news came that gave them hope: A peace agreement had been signed between North and South. The civil war, which had claimed more than two million lives, was over. The tenuous peace held, and in 2011 southern Sudan held a referendum in which its people almost unanimously decided to secede from Sudan and form a new nation.

Some of the Lost Boys were among the many thousands of South Sudanese refugees who streamed home during these optimistic years. They were eager to use their education to help build the world's newest independent country. One of them, Abraham Awolich, told The New York Times: "I don't want to see another generation of children go through what I've gone through and what other children of my generation went through." 2013 another war broke out between South Sudan President Salva Kiir and ex-President Riek Machar. The war and violence continue for four in half years. Salva Kiir and Riek Machar signed the final cease-fire and powersharing agreement in August 2018.

SURVEY THREE

John Garang De Mabior Quote

"Our struggle for **dignity, freedom, democracy,** and **good governance**. Our struggle for **justice** and **equality** for all -irrespective of their tribes, ethnic group, race religion or gender are indications that nobody is anybody's majority, and nobody is anyone's minority.

Dinka Leader John Garang

Kofi Piesie

I want to acknowledge and dedicate this Vol 4 to John Garang de Mabior, who is a member of the Dinka ethnic group. The Dinka people are warriors, so I get why this brother stood up and fought back against the Arabs in the Sudan. John Garang is regarded as the founding father and symbol of unity in today's South Sudan. Dr. John Garang coined the philosophy of "Sudanism," which would be the guiding philosophy to a secular and multiethnic New Sudan. Basically, the new Sudan is a concept for restructuring the Sudanese state, which the Sudan People's Liberation Army/ Movement proposed during the Second Sudanese Civil War. According to Mawut Achiecque Mach Guarak book Integration and Fragmentation of the Sudan: An African Renaissance, the original SPLA/M Manifesto outlined 'New Sudan' as a proposed united and secular Sudanese state. The vision of 'New Sudan' was developed by Dr. John Garang, who advocated the 'New Sudan' as a democratic and pluralistic state.

Dr. John Garang was a Sudanese politician and revolutionary leader. From 1983 to 2005, he led the Sudan People's Liberation Army during the Second Sudanese Civil War, and later, he served briefly as the vice president of the Sudan. This started out as a small acknowledgment page for the Dinka warrior Dr. John Garang but now has turn into a small chapter. I am going to go back and walk you through the life of this Dinka warrior. On June 23, 1945, John Garang was born to poor ethnic Dinka parents in Sudan's Wangulei village. His parents died when he was just ten years old, and he was educated at elementary schools in Wau and Rumbek, by a close relative. In 1962 John Garang joined the first Sudanese civil war, but because he was so young, the leaders encouraged him and others his age to seek an education. Because of the ongoing fighting, Garang was forced to complete his secondary education in Tanzania. After winning a scholarship, he went on to earn a Bachelor of Arts degree in Economics in 1969 from Grinnell College in Iowa, United States.

He was offered another scholarship to pursue graduate studies at the University of California, Berkeley, but he chose to return to Tanzania and study East African agricultural economics as a Thomas J. Watson Fellow at the University of Dar es Salaam (UDSM). At UDSM, he was a member of the University Students' African Revolutionary Front, and this is where he gains his interest in activism. However, Garang soon decided to return to Sudan and join the rebels. The civil war ended with the Addis Ababa Agreement of 1972, and Garang, like many rebels, was absorbed into the Sudanese military. For eleven years, he was a career soldier and rose from the rank of captain to colonel after taking the Infantry Officers Advanced Course at Fort Benning, Georgia, United States. During this period, he took four years of academic leave and received a Master's degree in agricultural economics from Iowa State University

(ISU). In 1981, he earned a PhD in Economics from Iowa State University (ISU).

By 1983, Col. Garang served as a senior instructor in the military academy in Wadi Sayedna, 21 km from the center of Omdurman, where he instructed the cadets for more than four years. Later he was nominated to serve in the military research department at Army HQ in Khartoum. Lieutenant Colonel John Garang of the SPAF was sent to quell a mutiny in Bor of 500 southern troops who were resisting orders to be relocated to the north. Instead of ending the mutiny, Garang encouraged mutinies in other garrisons and set himself at the head of the rebellion against the Khartoum government. When the government attacked Bor in May, and the battalion pulled out, Garang rode by an alternative route to join them in the rebel stronghold in Ethiopia. By the end of July, Garang had brought over 3000 rebel soldiers under his control through the newly created Sudan People's Liberation Army/Movement (SPLA/M), which was opposed to military rule and Islamic dominance of the country and encouraged other army garrisons to mutiny against the Islamic law imposed on the country by the government. William Nyuon Bany and Kerubino Kwanyin Bol were both founding members of SPLA. Bany was appointed the 3rd high-ranking Commander after Bol.

Garang was a strong advocate for national unity: minorities together formed a majority and therefore should rule. Together, Garang believed they could replace President Omar al-Bashir with a government made up of representatives from "all tribes and religions in Sudan." See right there, John Garang was about unity, so it didn't matter what background, what ethnic group you belong to, or religion. His first real effort for the cause, under his command, occurred in July 1985 with the SPLA's incursion into Kordofan. (Cockett, R., 2010, Sudan: Darfur and the Failure of an African State, Yale UP.) For many years the invaders had the government set up as one religion, one language, and for the most part, one dominant ethnic group ruling with primarily their own administrative office.

The SPLA gained the backing of Libya, Uganda, and Ethiopia. Garang and his army controlled a large part of the country's southern regions, named "New Sudan." He claimed his troops' courage came from "the conviction that we are fighting a just cause. That is something North Sudan and its people don't have." Critics suggested financial motivations to his rebellion, noting that much of Sudan's oil wealth lies in the south of the country. (Cockett, R., 2010, Sudan: Darfur and the Failure of an African State, Yale UP.) In the spring of 1991, Mengistu Haile Mariam's regime (in Ethiopia) was overthrown by the Khartoum backed Ethiopian rebels (Ethiopian People's Revolutionary Democratic Front). Upon the rebels' seizure of the government, they closed all SPLA training camps in Ethiopia and cut off the SPLA's arms supply, forcing the SPLA to return hundreds of thousands of Sudanese back to South Sudan. This disrupted military operations and leadership within the SPLA.

However, this caused the West to reconsider relations with the SPLA – justifying their providing the SPLA with "non-lethal help." (Flint, J. and Alex de Waal, 2008 (2nd Edn), Darfur: A New History of a Long War, Zed Books.) Shortly after, there was an attempted coup to oust Garang by senior SPLA commanders, Riek Machar and Lam Akol, in August 1991. The splinter group led by Machar and Akol was named the SPLA-Nasir. The coup turned out to be premature – however, it did expose the deep ethnic divides within the SPLA. When I read Riek Machar was attempting a coup on John Garang, it did not surprise me because Reik Marchar is a member of Nuer ethnic group, and John Garang is a member of the Dinka ethnic group. Both groups have been revival tribes for centuries. Later in this chapter, you will see Riek Machar is the cause of another civil war in the Sudan.

The Southern Sudanese communities became more divided than ever before in their history. These organic divides among the Southern Sudanese communities were exacerbated by the deliberate "divide and rule" policies instituted by the regimes in Khartoum to maintain their power over the Southern Sudanese peoples. SPLA-Nasir accused Garang of ruling by force, in a "dictatorial reign of terror"; but ethnic rivalry seemed to have a part, with the Nasir faction mainly composed of Nuer, and Garang's supporters mainly Dinka people. Months of fighting between the two factions left thousands dead in early 1992.The SPLA-Nasir also raised the idea of an independent south (whereas Garang wanted unity). (Banks, A.S.; Day,

A.J.; Muller, T.C. (2016). Political Handbook of the World 1998)

On September 14 1992, Bany, who was at the time Deputy Commander-in-Chief of the SPLA and Deputy Chairman of the SPLM, announces he is abanding his positions and association from the SPLA, and then escaped Garang territory. The following day, Commander Salva Kiir Mayardit was promoted from Chief of Staff to Bany's old positions of Deputy Commander-in-Chief and Deputy Chairman. Bany joined forces with Machar and Akol, and later joined forces with Bol to form SPLA-United, Sudanese People's Liberation Army-United. ("The National Courier: TODAY IN HISTORY: William Nyuon Bany, on September 27 1992, Defects from SPLA/M In Pageri) The SPLA and government signed a peace agreement on January 9, 2005, in Nairobi, in Kenya. On July 9, 2005, he was sworn in as the First-Vice-President - the second most powerful person in the country - following a ceremony in which he and President Omar al-Bashir signed a power-sharing constitution. Simultaneously, he became the premier in southern Sudan. This administration had limited autonomy for six years, at the end of which there would be a scheduled referendum regarding secession. No Christian or southerner had ever held such a high government post. Commenting after this ceremony, Garang stated, "I congratulate the Sudanese people; this is not my peace or the peace of al-Bashir, it is the peace of the Sudanese people."

Death and Legacy

Only a few months after the peace agreement, on July 30, 2005, a helicopter carrying Garang back from talks with the president of Uganda crashed in the mountains near the border. Although both Al-Bashir's government and Salva Kiir Mayardit, the new leader of the SPLM, blamed the crash on poor visibility, doubts remain about the crash. His legacy is that he is considered to be a very influential figure in the history of South Sudan. (Boddy-Evans, Alistair. "Biography of John Garang de Mabior." Oct. 23, 2020.) Let me elaborate a little more in-depth on the great Dinka leader death. Other reports I read states that when Dr. John Garang helicopter crash from returning from a meeting in Rwakitura with long-time ally President Yoweri Museveni of Uganda. He did not tell the Sudanese government that he was going to this meeting and therefore did not take the presidential plane. Dr. John Garang had told everyone he was going to spend the weekend in New Cush, a small village near the Kenyan borders founded by John Garang himself. To this day, neither the identity of any other participants at the meeting nor its purpose is known.

After the helicopter had been missing for more than 24 hours, the Ugandan president notified the Sudanese government, which in turn contacted the SPLM for information. The SPLM responded that the helicopter Garang was taking had landed safely on an old SPLA training camp. The Sudanese state television duly reported this. A few hours later, Abdel Basset Sabdarat, Sudan's

Information Minister, then appeared on TV to refute the earlier report that Garang's helicopter landed safely. It was, in fact, Yasir Arman, the SPLA/M spokesperson, who had told the government that Garang's plane had landed safely and his intention, in doing so, was to buy time for internal succession arrangements within the SPLA, before Garang's death was to be declared. Garang's helicopter crashed on Friday, and he remained 'missing' throughout Saturday. During this time, the government believed he was still resolving his affairs in Southern Sudan. Finally, a statement released by the office of the Sudanese President, Omar el-Bashir, confirmed that the Ugandan presidential helicopter had crashed into "a mountain range in southern Sudan because of poor visibility and this resulted in the death of Dr. John Garang DeMabior, six of his colleagues and seven Ugandan crew members." Yes there were lots of rumors flying around about Dr, John Garang death. Both the Sudanese government and the head of the SPLA blamed the weather for the accident. There are, however, doubts as to whether this was the true cause, especially among the rank and file of the SPLA. Yoweri Museveni, the Ugandan President, stated that the possibility of "external factors" having played a role could not be eliminated.

Before I end this chapter, I mention few names in this chapter like Salva Kiir Mayardit, who became Commander–in–Chief of Sudan People's Liberation Army(SPLA) following the death of Dr. John Garang, and Riek Machar, who was also a member and Commander of Sudan

Liberation Army (SPLA). Riek Machar was the one who tried to stage a violent coup to oust Dr. John Garang but was not successful. Keep in mind Riek Machar was from the Nuer people, whose tribe always had rivals with Dinka. Riek had an issue with John Garang, who was a Dinka, and then later with Salva Kirr, who was also Dinka. While Salva Kirr was President of South Sudan Riek Machar was his Vice President. The Sudanese all fought together to defeat Europeans and Arabs; who had taken over their country and control their government, which cause two civil wars,Sudanese against the foreigners. But later, there was a third civil war which now Sudanese against Sudanese.

Background

In December 2013, following a political struggle between Kiir and Machar that led to Machar's removal as vice president, violence erupted between presidential guard soldiers from the two largest ethnic groups in South Sudan. Soldiers from the Dinka ethnic group aligned with Kiir and those from the Nuer ethnic group supported Machar. Amid chaos, Kiir announced that Machar had attempted a coup and violence spread quickly to Jonglei, Upper Nile, and Unity states. From the outbreak of conflict, armed groups targeted civilians along ethnic lines, committed rape and sexual violence, destroyed property, and looted villages, and recruited children into their ranks.

South Sudan is not unfamiliar with violent wars. A region vastly differing from the rest of Sudan, South Sudan was always Christian and more aligned with Africa south of the Sahara while whereas Sudan which was overwhelmingly Muslim, identified with other Muslim nations of North Africa and the Middle East. This difference led to a push for independence from South Sudan and multiple civil wars. The most recent civil war ended in 2005 and led up to the referendum for independence in 2011 making South Sudan in 2018 the newest country in the world. Under the threat of international sanctions and following several rounds of negotiations supported by the Intergovernmental Authority on Development (IGAD), Kiir signed a peace agreement with Machar in August 2015. As the first step toward ending the civil war, Machar returned to Juba in April 2016 and was once again sworn in as vice president, after spending more than two years outside of the country. Soon after his return, violence broke out between government forces and opposition factions, once more displacing tens of thousands of people. Machar fled the country and was eventually detained in South Africa. In 2017 and 2018, a series of cease-fires were negotiated and subsequently violated between the two sides and other factions.

After almost five years of civil war, Kiir and Machar participated in negotiations mediated by Uganda and Sudan in June 2018. Later that month, Kiir and Machar signed the Khartoum Declaration of Agreement that included a cease-fire and a pledge to negotiate a power-sharing agreement to end the war. Despite sporadic violations over the ensuing weeks, Kiir and Machar signed a final cease-fire and power-sharing agreement in August 2018. This agreement was followed by a peace agreement to end the civil war signed by the government and Machar's opposition party, along with several other rebel factions. The agreement, called the Revitalized Agreement on the Resolution of the Conflict in South Sudan, included a new power-sharing structure and reinstated Machar as vice president. In late October 2018, Machar returned to South Sudan for a nationwide peace celebration to mark the end of the civil war. However, reports of continued attacks and violations, coupled with the collapse of multiple previous peace deals, highlight concerns that the fragile peace may not hold. Although official casualties are difficult to confirm, one April 2018 study estimated that nearly four hundred thousand people were killed during the five years of war, an additional nearly four million were internally displaced or fled the country.

Part II (Combat)

Surveying the Spear Masters

T'challa Bangoura

I write these words in the most serious, determined, and focused of moods. As technology would have it, my entire first draft for this volume was corrupted and unrecoverable. Starting fresh and irritated beyond words, I am in the perfect mood for some spear play. This survey is from the perspective of one who studies the art of movement, defense mechanisms, and overall behavior during combat among our species and various other life forms. As stated in my survey for vol.3, I have combined many techniques and incorporated them to make unique workouts and have come up with a style of combat that has proven to be as effective as it is unorthodox. The techniques we will focus on are various styles of combat using the spear. We will primarily focus on three types of spear play coming from the Northern Shaolin Temple, and two masters on the beautiful continent of Afrika, like the Ama Zulu, the Maasai. I will conclude with a workout regimen to show what I do to stay in shape, and how I incorporate vital lessons from warriors around the world. I want to start by examining the Northern Shaolin Temple.

The Northern Shaolin Temple and the six main forms:

Before we examine what is known as the "six main forms" using the spear, we are going to need some background on the Shaolin in order to properly understand the history, psychology, and motivation behind such an extremely effective school of discipline as it pertains to the arts and specifically spear play. It is impossible to begin this journey without understanding at least the surface level of history behind the Shaolin and their teachings. Here is a small passage from https://www.thoughtco.com/history-of-the-shaolin-monks-195814:

"By Kallie Szczepanski

Updated April 20, 2019

The Shaolin Monastery is the most famous temple in China, renowned for its kung fu fighting Shaolin monks. With amazing feats of strength, flexibility, and pain-endurance, the Shaolin have created a worldwide reputation as the ultimate Buddhist warriors. Yet Buddhism is generally considered to be a peaceful religion with an emphasis on principles such as non-violence, vegetarianism, and even self-sacrifice to avoid harming others — how, then, did the monks of Shaolin Temple become fighters? The history of Shaolin begins about 1500 years ago, when a stranger arrived in China from lands to the west, bringing with him a new interpretation of religion, and it spans to modern-day China, where tourists from around the world come to experience displays of their ancient martial arts and teachings.

Origin of the Shaolin Temple

Legend says that around 480 CE, a wandering Buddhist teacher came to China from India, known as Buddhabhadra, Batuo, or Fotuo in Chinese. According to later, Chan — or in Japanese, Zen — Buddhist tradition, Batuo taught that Buddhism could best be transmitted from master to student rather than through the study of Buddhist texts. In 496, the Northern Wei Emperor Xiaowen gave Batuo funds to establish a monastery at holy Mt. Shaoshi in the Song Mountain range, 30 miles from the imperial capital of Luoyang. This temple was named Shaolin, with "Shao" taken from Mount Shaoshi and " lin" meaning "grove" — however, when Luoyang and the Wi Dynasty fell in 534, temples in the area were destroyed possibly including Shaolin. Another Buddhist teacher was Bodhidharma, who came from either India or Persia. He famously refused to teach Huike, a Chinese disciple, and Huike cut off his own arm to prove his sincerity, becoming the Bodhidharma's first student as a result. The Bodhidharma also reportedly spent nine years in silent meditation in a cave above Shaolin, and one legend says that he fell asleep after seven years and cut off his own eyelids so that it could not happen again — the eyelids turned into the first tea bushes when they hit the soil."

We can see many conceptual ideas and mythological explanations; however, the basic principles and traditions stand firm. Part of a monk's peaceful nature comes from the Buddhist teachings from western lands, as mentioned; however, there is another side to Wushu art forms. In nature, every living organism must be able to defend itself from predators and the elements. Our species have observed the nature of life for quite some time, and eventually, we create different ways to use the spear based on our influences in the environment. One life form comes to mind almost immediately when studying the arts and specifically spear play, and that is the tiger. Many styles of combat have emerged, both armed and unarmed, from observing such powerful and dominant creatures of the Eastern lands of China. One such form is the Five tiger Spear, which will be the first of three styles we focus on. This form of spear belongs to a group of styles with five other forms that are the six main forms of spear play. Five Tiger style generally uses a standard spear length that is between 9-14 ft. and focuses on explosive and powerful movements to mimic the tiger. There are many forward thrusts, and well-balanced/ low stance strikes to generate power. We refer to this as 'sitting down on your punches" in the world of combat sports. This is when an individual will be in a slightly deeper squat stance, having a lower center of gravity creating angles and distance for momentum to travel. All tiger forms require these basic techniques, and therefore one must have discipline and strengthen their body to utilize the style effectively.

Moving on to the Liu He Da Qiang/ Liu He Spear. Da(big/ giant) Qiang(lance) is usually translated as "six harmonies great spear." The Ming Dynasty had its reign up until 1644 AD. Still, during this time, the military primarily used this weapon, and civilians who took an interest were often young men planning to join the military. The "great lance" is far too long and heavy to be used practically due to the overall length being at least 3-4 meters, even up to 5 in some cases, and the shaft is made out of hard and sturdy wood for support of its length. "Right off the rip," as our dear brother Kofi Piesie would say, we see this particular spear is intended for long-range combat. The first thing that comes to mind is core stability, footwork, overall strength, and conditioning, topping it all off with superb focus. Wielding a spear with at least 6-8 extra inches of length compared to other spears would be too taxing on the body if not properly trained resulting in immediate defeat.

 Exercises that would help prepare one for such a taxing endeavor would be horse stance, practicing the five basic kicks (ten thousand reps each), shoulder strengthening exercises, all abdominal strengthening exercises, especially for the spinal erectors. These are but a few crucial movements to be familiar with when focusing on Liu He spear play. Movements with this style are not as explosive and flashy as Five Tiger and other styles, however, the marksmanship/accuracy one can achieve with a weapon yielding such a long reach is unmatched. Once again, we can see the advantages of athletes with a longer reach usually perform better, contacting their opponent faster than their opponent can reach them. There are exceptions to the rule, such as athletes like the G.O.A.T. Muhammad Ali, and superbly talented Saul Canelo Alvarez; they seem to have a way of nullifying an opponent's attributes no matter how long of a reach or size of a fighter. However, we are focused on reach as it pertains to spear play, and it is a bit more complicated dodging a spear than it is a punch.

We now move to our third style, the Double Spear. Out of the six main styles using spears among the Northern Shaolin disciplines, this style is undoubtedly tricky because facing this opponent means there are two spears to watch for. As a martial arts enthusiast, this style of spear play falls in my top 3 favorites. Mental fortitude is a must when using a technique that requires a single weapon in each hand, and it adds an entire world of dynamics to combat. I can also speak to this as a musician when teaching students of all ages and skill levels. For instance, the fact that students who have a Ph.D. in music will still have issues doing basic exercises that require both hands to operate at times in unison and at other times separately while maintaining a particular part in the rhythm. Much is the same in technique with Shaolin Wushu and the double spear, dividing a single shaft into two separate sections, creating lightning-fast and seemingly unbeatable formations. Single thrusts pose the threat of another strike, while speed is increased due to the range of mobility being increased now that the two upper limbs can operate independently. There is a saying that is known throughout the martial world, "one hand lies, the other tells the truth." We refer to this as the "sleight of hand," and it is most certainly used throughout the world of combat sports. One uses the jab in order to find range and to provide a distraction while looking to land a decent shot. Keeping your opponent's focus on the "pawing jab" and throwing the hook to finish off the combination. Encounters between warriors are thought to be 80/20 or 90/10 in a mental/physical ratio; if one does not have the mental capacity for warfare, one should not seek to engage in combat.

Before we move any further, I want to take a moment to ponder what we have observed so far. We have so many rich traditions from around the globe that utilize the spear in some form or fashion. Entire civilizations have thrived from living a simple and healthy lifestyle with this tool as their main source of protection, hunting capabilities. In some cases, it can be the walking stick needed in old age; given that these complex styles have emerged from the genius of our species, we need to consider how we got here. How did this 400,000 years old piece of technology become one of the most crucial tools in our survival even to this day? Which stories have we yet to hear? Which of our ancestors has been forgotten? When do we allow those without a voice to speak? Perhaps we may find an answer to these questions, far away from these lands, across the Himalayas, to a land that is home to the oldest spear masters, and to the ancestors of our species, Afrika.

Surveying Afrika: Ama Zulu, Maasai, Applying the Wisdom

The Ama Zulu is probably one of the most known Afrikan nations, and they probably come to mind due to the classic leopard skin cloths and spear-wielding warriors. Spears are of the utmost importance across many nations on the continent. The Ama Zulu (and neighboring people such as the Nguni) primarily use a long throwing spear known as an assegai. Several of these spears may be carried at a time, as well as a bow and cowhide shield. King Shaka Zulu used technology already forged and in use across the southern regions with a different, more close-combat-practical version of the spear known as iklwa/ umkhwa, and it would play a crucial role in his reign as king. He seemingly popularized it as he fought to secure a legacy of his own against the real enemy of the day, the British.

There are tales that say he may have learned about this "short-stabbing" spear from his cousin Makhedama who had implemented the iklwa for his regiments. When Shaka came into power, the spear was well known and used to attack fleeing enemies by most neighboring villages. Nonetheless, he was a warrior of innovation, adaptation, and revolution as he focused on stopping the "in fighting" or "Dwenemen" as the Akan West Africa says. Whether or not he invented/ popularized the iklwa continues to be examined and discussed. The use of these spears would continue long after his death, and by this point in history, the concept of adaptation with the need for several types of spears within a single culture would ultimately emerge for many people around the world.

So far, we have identified five variations of spear masters. We see how dear the Shaolin Temple regards them as the "king of all weapons," and the Ama Zulu, along with numerous neighboring relative people, make good use of their variations. What good is this information to me, the author of these words, and you, the reader? The answer is simple, HEALTH. The lifestyles of the groups mentioned above have proven up until this day that living our daily lives with an emphasis on exercise, eating healthy, and staying active boosts your chances of living longer. Not to mention the moral values that are shared are exactly what we need in the world today.

I personally take a slice from each of these spear masters pertaining to philosophy, mental sharpness, martial prowess, physical strengthening, and overall peace of mind. Life has a way of humbling you, reminding you that no matter how "modern" we get, we should always be able to fend for ourselves and not rely on running water and electricity when these things can be gone in an instant. From the natural disaster survivors of hurricanes, tornados, and wildfires to the people being ordered to evacuate apartment complexes due to poor/outdated engineering. We must be able to survive if such things occur and honor our ancestors by at least keeping the traditions alive. If we cannot survive without the artificial, how can we cry for the organic?

The Maasai

Reigning in the rift valley, herding cattle, and dueling with lions, the Maasai (meaning speakers of the Maa language) are certainly some of the fiercest warriors known to man. They are situated on the borders of Kenya and Tanzania. Each day the warriors are expected to protect the village against invaders and predators. To do this, the young Maasai or layok must have their initiation ceremony and pass several tests in order to be established as a young man and complete the journey from boy-manhood, becoming what they call moran. One of such tests is that each young boy must slay a lion to show his bravery and prepare him for the daily possibility of stopping a lion from attacking the village. Imagine a lion carrying off a sibling because you were too afraid to thrust it with your spear and defend your village's peace? Much is to be said about the man who faces the lion with nothing but his heart and the point of his spear.

Each Maasai patrols the village with their turkana or spear in one hand and shield in the other. There is absolutely no running around the village with an unsheathed spear, randomly poking people, or objects, nor do we find issues with mass murder using these deadly weapons on their own community. All warriors would properly deal with anyone who would lose their character. This speaks to the responsibility that one has as a protector, a spear master of whom an entire village depends on for survival. There is no time for crimes against the village, horseplay, or silly disputes when hungry predators such as raiders, hyenas, and lions wait for you to let your guard down for just one moment so they can launch their attack. They have no running water or electricity, yet they live a simple and peaceful lifestyle. Some of our most disciplined and fiercest warriors look after cattle and seek to be harmonious with their environment.

Applying the Wisdom(mind)

I briefly spoke to the physical applications of these various spear masters and their practical benefits to those who live a different lifestyle. It is important to keep in mind that the mental aspect of applying said wisdom is the toughest part. I have framed the next part of this survey with the sections being labeled with names of specific striking techniques with the spear, allowing me to focus on the everlasting battle of life as we all strive to create, protect, and enjoy it to the best of our abilities.

Thrust forward in your daily endeavors armed with the knowledge and objective understanding of yesterday's problems, applying today's solutions, bringing about the change we need for tomorrow. Find time within your day to educate yourself about yourself. Learn what foods cause inflammation and other complications and limit them. Would you please start thinking about the future of your legacy, meaning your bloodline, and how the food choices we make today ultimately affect our children and their children as well? Be forward-minded as you press through these difficult and confusing times. Ask for a demonstration of "suspect" information by providing a source of what is being disseminated. Like the relentless thrust of the Five Tiger Spear, press forward and challenge all data that "feels good."

Push back those who wish to downplay learning about new things for the sake of bettering your people. Push back on those who seek to downplay Afrika; after all, she has given and continues to give to the world. Take heed because the next moment is not promised and what once stood tall and strong could be taken away so quickly. The past few weeks marked a true milestone and breakthrough for me as I had to do these things and so much more. My daily routine consists of rising early to ground myself in Afrikan-ancestral thought, thrusting forward mentally with the motion of the Maasai spear as they thrust the heart of a lion or any deadly threat to their village. I symbolically thrust forward, piercing any negativity center mass and completely out of my head. Afterward, I will take myself through a workout that might look something like what I described in vol3, along with some extra strength and conditioning. I will find my way to the daily grind of earning a dollar and eventually write these words.

Sweep all negativity from the day aside and carve out some time to contribute to the liberation of Afrikan minds. Sweeping all the "you can't" or "you wish you could" comments and opinions into a big pile, then throw the whole thing away. We must sweep up all conspiracy theories and unsubstantiated claims, especially those detrimental to our health. Rid yourself of every reason why you won't make a better decision tomorrow, why you won't choose not to argue and fight with your spouse. Take all those feelings and drop them to the floor, sweep them into the pile. Take the time to appreciate the loved ones in your life and give them their roses while they can still smell them. Sweep away all the fake Moors who claim to be so educated about West Afrika into the pile, especially those that have the last name "Bey" and do nothing but block our good brother Sutkeh from commenting on their youtube vidoes, and sell travel stories, acting like North Afrikans from Morocco are the same as sub-Saharan West Afrikans.

Sweep the doubt and depression off your shoulders as we enter the second half of the year. Make the next six months count as we all strive to make this new lifestyle work. Don't let anyone stop you from starting a business, writing several books and reaching Afrika, getting a new job, buying a new house, etc. This is not the time to give in to the pressures of life but rather sweep them away. Focus on what you can do with what you have. All of this was done by our ancestors and is still done by our brothers and sisters on the continent and globally. Imagine staring at a lion across the plains, spear in hand, preparing for the imminent death of either it or yourself. There would be no time for hesitation or cowardness, for the village's future rests on the point of your spear.

Prick with the intellectual sharpness of a well-trained scholar. Look to our community with all the problems we have and point them in the direction of good information that has been proven to deliver results. Keep the pseudo claims and rhetoric at bay by pricking at their weak points. Poke tiny holes in their argument constantly to trip them up. Prick at the one point they can't explain. Be like a tag on the inside of a new shirt you forgot to rip off, constantly pricking at the side of your neck or underarm until you are driven insane and are forced to remove your shirt and properly deal with the nascence. Make them properly explain everything because we deserve nothing less. Prick at the lazy teachers who barely cover what is required in the handbooks. Prick all images of failure out of your head. Envision success and start taking the small steps needed to achieve it. With this motion, the Maasai keep the lions at bay, and the monks of the Shaolin Temple fought against raiders for generations.

Circles must be protected and often work best when they are tight. Your circle is your network, allowing you to connect with like-minded individuals just as we have here at Kofi Piesie Research Team. We should vet all whom we welcome into our circles. Do everything you can to find out if they are a good fit instead of just saying they are a good fit because you have a few things in common, or they may appear to have a place in your circle. Ask about their mission, their purpose in their work, and see if there is compatibility to the degree of harmony. Not all compatible candidates are harmonious. Circle a date on the calendar for every month to sit down and meet with various members of your network. Check-in with them often and ask if there is anything you can do to improve the relationship. People remember when we check-in and often circle back to you if they have drifted and grown distant. Please step back and examine your circle often, holding all those within (beginning with yourself) accountable to maintaining its structural integrity.

All must follow suit, including us, KPRT, and all of you who support our work, making you a part of our circle. We are all connected and play our role in making sure we give our babies a better fighting chance than we had. Encircle the enemy and their misinformation, like the Ama Zulu and their beautifully intimidating dance that startled and confused the much deserving British. We will surround their pseudo ideas and let our sourced-up spears fly!

Applying the Wisdom(body)

There are a couple of points within this survey where I mention the workout regimen I put forth in vol. 3. Below is a modified version implementing the disciplines outlined in this survey. The purpose is to promote health and wellness, especially during the time of a pandemic. Take caution, check your ego at the door, and remember that "slow and steady wins the race."

Warm-up of your choice	15 min. minimal water	Mandatory/daily
5 Tiger Stye Thrust	2min. 60 sec rest, repeat	5 sets (adjust as needed)
Horse stance 100 kicks	Duration is skill based	Twice during training
Double spear formations	Duration is skill based	10 sets (adjust as needed)

5 Tiger Stye Thrust	Aim for power/ 1min rest	5 sets (adjust as needed)
Abdominal exercises	High reps/ 1 min rest	4 sets (adjust as needed)
Deep breathing exercises	2 min/ 30 sec rest	3 sets (performed daily)
Cool down/ reflection	Meditation/stillness	20 min (performed daily)

As we observe the table, we see that this training session immediately demands mental and physical discipline. This is so that we can apply the wisdom and boost our chances of avoiding unnecessary conflict. We thrust forward and look to a brighter tomorrow with a fresh workout:

Warm up of your choice	15 min. minimal water	Mandatory/ daily
200 bodyweight squat	Perform 50 squats prior to resting/ 1min	2 sets (may be split up over the workout)
100 jabs, 100 uppercuts	Aim for speed/ 1min rest	3 sets (adjust as needed)
100 roundhouse kicks	Focus on form/ 2 min rest	3 sets (adjust as needed)

Liu He Spear formations	20 min/ 2 min rest	Performed twice
Circle, Sweep, Prick (strikes with spear)	50 strikes each, 30 min/ 2 min rest	Performed once
Capoeira Jinga	10 min no rest	Performed twice
Cool down/ reflection	Meditation/stillness	20 min (performed daily)

The heart, mind, and body of a warrior must reflect unwavering tenacity and must be battle-tested to defend one's peace properly. We conclude with the final workout to this entire routine, completely shocking the body and confusing the muscles, performed on the third day:

Warm up of your choice	15 min. minimal water	Mandatory/ daily
Front and side Kicks (performed in horse stance)	200 reps each/ 2 min rest	Performed once
Hold various 5 Tiger formation stances	Hold each form for 5 min/2 min rest	Perform each formation twice

Djembe speed drill	Revisit vol 3 for details	Performed twice
Spar with a partner (if possible no matter the style)	15 rounds/ 1min rest in between	Performed once per week
Jump kicks(any variation)	15 min/ 2 min rest in between	Performed twice
Cardio of any type	30 min straight without rest	Performed at the end of training
Cool down/ reflection	Meditation/stillness	20 min (performed daily)

Provided you haven't passed out from exhaustion, take a moment to reflect on all that has been given. Ask yourself if you have given your all in every task. Work hard, rest well, and be consistent!

Part III (History)

SURVEY FIVE

AAVE & Code Switching: Products of the Influence Acculturation and Assimilation

Chavis Tp-hsb Ahaw McCray

Did acculturation and assimilation breed the phenomenon of African American Vernacular English and code switching? This essay is an attempt to objectively analyze some the available data and see what can be deduced. What inspired this topic was 2 books that I read in the past couple years. One was "Nsw.t Bjt.j (king) in Ancient Egyptian: A Lesson in Paronymy and Leadership" by Asar Imhotep. The other "The Developmental Psychology of the Black Child" by Dr. Amos Wilson. Though the title may sound unrelated you would be amazed what kind of substance you can extract from the monumental minds of these 2 dynamic authors as their scientifically grounded Afrocentric methodological and scholarly approach to researching the Afrikan Worldview and mind is second to none based on my personal opinion formed via reading multiple of publications of which I own and plan to pass down to my sons, family, and community due to the works being so versatile and powerfully inspiring and motivating Both publications took the time linguistically examine our people in great detail. The mere vocabulary and sources used by these authors will open the door to concepts you would never fathom to look in to and further research or talk about in our community collectively. A publication Asar recommends is "African Voices: An Introduction to the

Languages of Africa" by Vic Webb and Kembo- Sure. It is a very informative book that offers college level linguistic competence on our people language. Ir actually defines code switching as "language alternation across sentence boundaries" (Webb. V, Sure. Pg.92, 2000) Chandra D.L. Waring in an internet article elaborates further on code switching when she states "Code-switching is the practice of interacting in different ways depending on the social context, and it isn't limited to race. Most of us interact differently when hanging out with friends than we would during a job interview.

However, due in large measure to structural inequality and centuries of segregation, different cultural norms and ways of speaking have emerged among white and Black Americans.

But because dominant culture is White, whiteness has been baked into institutions as natural, normal and legitimate. So, there's much more incentive for people of color to code-swich – to adapt to the dominant culture to improve their prospects. White people rarely, if ever, feel this same pressure in their daily lives." (Waring, C, 2018) The first thing that needs to be done is define the terms at play to fully comprehend the concept of code switching to form an even greater grasp using one more source directly dealing the subject which says "Code switching (also code-switching, CS) is the practice of moving back and forth between two languages or between two dialects or registers of the same language at one time. Code switching occurs far more often in conversation than in writing. It is also called code-mixing and style-shifting. It is studied by linguists to examine when people do it, such as under what circumstances do bilingual speakers switch from one to another, and it is studied by sociologists to determine why people do it, such as how it relates to their belonging to a group or the surrounding context of the conversation (casual, professional, etc.)

"Code-switching performs several functions (Zentella, 1985). First, people may use code-switching to hide fluency or memory problems in the second language (but this accounts for about only 10 percent of code switches). Second, code-switching is used to mark switching from informal situations (using native languages) to formal situations (using the second language). Third, code-switching is used to exert control, especially between parents and children. Fourth, code-switching is used to align speakers with others in specific situations (e.g., defining oneself as a member of an ethnic group). Code-switching also 'functions to announce specific identities, create certain meanings, and facilitate particular interpersonal relationships' (Johnson, 2000, p. 184)." (William B. Gudykunst, Bridging Differences: Effective Intergroup Communication, 4th ed. Sage, 2004)" (Nordquist, R. 2020)

In Asar's work mentioned (Imhotep, 2016) in chapter 1 pg. 56 and beyond he touches on "Secret and Play languages" of different tribes essentially demonstrating multiple examples of code switching across Africa that verify the various functions quoted above. This suggests code switching is just a part of African culture. Engrained in the societal psyche employed for a plethora of reasons. But that doesn't omit more modern dynamics of the concept that Waring addresses in her article specifically mentioning the switch made by blacks when interacting with whites. In her article titled "What Is Code-Switching and Why Do Black Americans Do It?" she assesses benefit and consequence of the linguistic phenomenon via testimony of blacks themselves expressing their responses ranging from interviewees bragging about their ability to code-switch: "To some people, I'll say 'He was handsome!' versus 'He fine as hell, girl!' And I think I'm the baddest because I can talk to this group and that group in the same way that they talk." to "One participant in my study told me that he is perpetually self-conscious about code-switching out of fear that someone would witness his behavior and question his authenticity." (Waring, C. 2018) If we prod this dynamic with our sociological curiosity, we find ourselves asking what the interviewee was benefiting from and why did the other feel self-conscious about their behavior. What is going on here? I think now is the perfect time to introduce ACCULTURATION into the assessment and refer back to Dr. Wilson and Vic Webb publication where insight is given to offer psychological and sociolinguistic perspective necessary to see how acculturation plays a role. Webb defines sociolinguistic as "the study of language is in relation to society" expounding further "the study of society- its structured belief, traditions and practices belong to the discipline of sociology, and sociolinguistics is thus a hybrid discipline which combines sociological and linguistic concepts and techniques to study the role of function of language society." (Webb. V, Sure. Pg.92, 2000).

Wilson utilizes this approach in chapter 7 pg. 177 breaking down the sociocultural basis of language behavior stating " it is obvious to even the most casual observer that different races and nationalities speak differently that within races and nations, language and dialect differ according to region and cultural, class and educational backgrounds. Yet as we have documented in the foregoing section, no one is born speaking or born with a special predisposition to speak exclusively one particular language or only in his "mother tongue". For apparent adaptive reasons than human neonate is born with the capacity for learning to speak any language it is exposed to for a certain period of time consequently regardless of race the infant is capable of learning with equal ease any language he is exposed to for the first 94 to 5 years of life" (Wilson, A. 2014) The language relevant to our discussion that Blacks in America learn is English. An article significant to our discussion defines Acculturation as "a process through which a person or group from one culture comes to adopt the practices and values of another culture, while still retaining their own distinct culture. This process is most commonly discussed regarding a minority culture adopting elements of the majority culture, as is typically the case with immigrant groups that are culturally or ethnically distinct from the majority in the place to which they have immigrated." (Cole, N. 2020). The so called "immigrant" here is the African American. Blacks are the minority forced to accept the English language striped of their native languages forced to assimilate. Kole clarifies the difference stating "Acculturation is not the same as the process of assimilation, though some people use the words interchangeably. Assimilation can be an eventual outcome of the acculturation process, but the process can have other outcomes as well, including rejection, integration, marginalization, and transmutation." (Cole, N. 2020). English was assimilated into the African mind via slavery in case you have been under a rock the past 400 years and was not aware. On pg 178 Wilson gives a brief history of the black dialect which we could argue equates ro AAVE describing " black American dialects are probably the result of creolized form of English, at one time spoken on the southern plantations by black slaves. This creolized plantation English appears to be related to the creolized English spoken by some blacks in Jamaica other Caribbean islands. Through the interaction with white speech the black dialect can no longer be considered true Creole dialects, but still, they maintain many Creole features structural characteristics. African who were captured as slaves and brought to the New World were forced to learn to use some type of English" (Wilson, A. 2014). In an article titled "The Limits of Standard English" explains AAVE as " a dialect no less complex or expressive than more prestigious forms of the language. It is rule-bound and systematic. It also happens to be the means of communication of a marginalized, often economically disadvantaged group of people. In fact, AAVE possesses at least one fine grammatical distinction that standard English completely lacks. Pullum explains that there is a "remote present perfect" tense in AAVE, evident in expressions like "she been married," where "been" is emphasized. This doesn't just mean "she has been married," but "she is married and has been for some considerable time.

"In a similar way, the AAVE form "be" + present participle — "be walking," "be singing," et cetera—is often mistaken for the equivalent of the English present continuous tense: "is walking," "is singing." In fact, it marks what is called "habitual aspect"—meaning the action is performed as a rule, not necessarily right this minute. "He sings" therefore means not "he is singing," but "he sings [as a hobby, or professionally]." (Shariatmadari, D. January 7, 2020). Here we see the resilience of the African American taking what is given to them and making it work for them. Retrofitting a foreign language into their paradigm and molding it into a new custom dialect. David substantiates our findings prior to this quote stating, "because this dialect is one that's very close to standard English and is used by a group whose status is generally low, it gets branded as "sloppy speaking," "slang," or "ghetto." The last label, although freighted with racial judgment, could at least make linguistic sense. We know that dialects emerge when there is geographical stasis. In areas of cities that are primarily black for a number of years, even decades, distinctive ways of speaking are likely to develop—more so given that the isolation is in this case both physical and social.

(Shariatmadari, D. January 7, 2020). Because AAVE is a dialect of the English language it is fair to conclude the assimilation into American culture through acculturation is what influenced this linguistic phenomenon we derogatorily recognize as "Ebonics". Wilson gets to the core of realistic consequences and conflicts on pg 186 where he demonstrates the essential struggle that starts in adolescence switching back and forth between standard English and what he calls the black dialect again equates AAVE. In this quote " in approaching standard English the black child as in the case with any nonstandard English-speaking child does not simply throw away his previous language experience that prior linguistic experience interferes with his efforts to read, write, and speak standard English" (Wilson, A. 2014). This hits home as this has always been something I personal dealt with as a kid to an adult. Retyping, rewriting, rephrasing sentences because I am psychologically hopping back and forth from proper English and AAVE code switching sometimes code mixing. Exposed to different subcultures (i.e., gang culture) and geographic locations (San Diego and Houston) codes expand far beyond simplistic ideas of black and white and acculturation. But we are with this thorough assessment able to see the influences acculturation followed by assimilation in AAVE and code switching as well as the innate human social and psychological response of creating codes and dialects to communicate effectively on multiple levels for survival and advancement.

SURVEY SIX

Sun Worship: Expanded Sun Gods

Setepenre Meri Amen

In this edition, I will be dealing with the Sun gods of man, expanding on my previous work done in Spearitual Combat. I talked about how early man venerated the Sun and its relationship with agriculture. History has shown us that human beings from various parts of the world have one thing in common: they worshiped the Sun. In the quest to understand how nature works, early cultures praised the Sun and did some things to appease the Sun so that it would continue to provide the earth with its rays. Some of these things include warfare, sacrifice, rituals, and monuments dedicated to the Sun. By the end of this survey, I hope the reader can use this as a reference when searching for Sun deities around the globe.

We will begin this survey in Africa with Anyawu Sun, god of the Igbo people. The name Anyawu means "Eye of light" in Igbo. It is a combination of two Igbo words, anya meaning eye, and anwu, meaning light which would be the literal meaning. But the Igbo also has a metaphorical meaning as one author states, "Metaphorically, this sight represents itself as insight, which is the capacity to gain an accurate and deep intuitive understanding of a person or thing, and foresight, the ability to predict what will happen or be needed in the future. In short, insight is the ability to see things as they really are, and foresight is the ability to see things as they will be. If this is the case, Anyawu was a deity that had the power to inspire insight and foresight in people." Nnadiebube Journal of Philosophy, Vol. 2 (2), 2018. A lot of Igbo people use Anyawu as their surname, and this is how much they revered the god.

Sun worship in ancient Kemet is centered around the god Re, born out of the waters of nun Re is said to have brought himself into existence. Re has many manifestations of himself; the people of Kemet known as Remetch dedicated monuments, cities, and many different offerings to Re so that he would return from the duat unscaved by Apep. "The Egyptians believed that each day the sun god was born. In the morning, after his bath and breakfast, he began his journey across the sky in his boat and would spend one hour inspecting each of his twelve provinces. When the Sun went down, Re was believed to enter the underworld until the morning when he was born again. All night long, the supreme god had to fight his enemy Apep, the terrible serpent of the underworld". (Storm 63) This constant struggle of good vs. evil is rooted in Egyptian mythology.

When we look at the sun deity of Sumeria, known as Utu, later known as Shamash, which is represented by the sun disc, he is known for justice, generosity, and affairs with man. Shamsh rode across the sky in his chariot every morning, bringing sustenance to the world until dusk, when it was then time to enter the underworld and judge the dead. "In primitive times, he was supposed to stride over the heavens on foot but in later times to do so in a fiery chariot which was drawn by animals driven by one Bunene.

He was regarded as a gracious God, for he helped all who were in trouble, gave life to the dead, and set free him that was in bonds. Possessing the power to see everywhere, he knew all things and judged men rightly." (85) His name is found in cuneiform text dating as far back as 3500 BCE in the form of Utu, then Shamash later on around 2600 BCE. One of them being The Epic of Gilgamesh, where he helps Gilgamesh defeat his enemies of the cedar forest. Mithra, the sun god of the Indo-Aryans, Persians, and even extended to the Romans empire, is said to be the god of contracts, friendship, and sunlight. As tradition states, Mithra rode across the sky in a golden chariot pulled by white horses bringing the rising Sun from the underworld. "According to one tradition, as the Sun, Mithra formed a link between Ahura Mazda and Angra Mainyu, the principle of darkness. This supposition was built on the understanding that the Sun marked the continual revolutions of light and dark". (Storm 50) The Romans worshipped Mithra by way of Cilician pirates who practiced the worship of Mithra; some scholars disagree. But when Rome expanded into Asia during Alexander the Great, Mitra was inevitably going to be practiced by them as they frequently adopted other cultures.

The Greeks believed in the sun god/titan Helios who was also the guardian of oaths and god of sight. When it comes to the Greeks, they did not revere the Sun as many other cultures did. So, in the pantheon of greek culture, Helios is not that high. Although Helios appears in many poems and literature did by Plato, Homer gives us a description in this hymn; "[Helios the Sun] rides his chariot, he shines upon men and deathless gods, and piercingly he gazes with his eyes from his golden helmet. Bright rays beam dazzlingly from him, and his bright locks streaming from the temples of his head gracefully enclose his far-seen face: a rich, fine-spun garment glows upon his body and flutters in the wind: and stallions carry him. Then, when he has stayed his golden-yoked chariot and horses, he rests there upon the highest point of heaven until he marvelously drives them down again through heaven to Okeanos (Oceanus)." Homeric Hymn 31 to Helius (trans. Evelyn-White) (Greek epic C7th - 4th B.C.)

The island of Rhodes did play a significant role in worshipping Helios due to the story of the nymph Rhodos who the island was named after bore him seven sons. In later Greek history, the people began to lean more towards Apollo as the Patreon sun god starting around the fifth century and even more during the Hellenistic period. Taking a look into the Hindu sun god Surya which is first mentioned in hymns of Rigveda as the rising Sun, and in other stories as an actual sun god, the origins differ in the Rigveda. Like the other sun gods, he also rode a chariot across the sky and fought off demons during the night.

During the thirteenth century, the people built a sandstone temple dedicated to Surya in the Orissa region at Konarak. "Surya is known by many alternative names and epithets, which include Vivasvat (Brilliant), Savitr (the Nourisher), Bhaskara (Light-maker), Dinakara (Day-maker),

Lokacaksuh (Eye of the World), Graharaja (King of the Constellations), and Sahasra-kirana (Of a 1,000 rays). Vishnu, who later largely replaces Surya's function in the Hindu pantheon, is referred to as Surya-Narayana in his incarnation as the Sun." (Cartwright 2016) We find that this is a common story; when time passes, people find new meaning and insight in what they believe is true and should be updated. Coming to the Americas, I like to start with the Mayans and their worship of the sun god Kinich Ahau also known as (God G), when studying the codex. The Mayans studied the Sun, tracked its movements across the sky, learned to tell time and predict solar events. "It is no coincidence then that the word for Sun, day and time are the same or are very similar to each other in all Mayan languages. To keep track of time, the Maya observed and recorded the yearly cycles of the Sun, including the times of equinoxes, solstices, and the zenith and nadir passages." (Smithsonian) Tho Kinich Ahau did not have a chariot like the sun gods of the far east, in the literature, it is said: "Kinich Ahau was the sun, and was believed to turn into a jaguar as he went through Xibalbá each night." In the form of the jaguar, Kinich Ahau would defeat his enemies to bring forth light.

The Aztecs, on the other hand, believed in multiple different sun gods for their multiple different creation stories. The Aztecs believe the five creation stories to be the various ages of man, and with each new age, a new sun god is needed. Originally a god of the night, Tezcatlipoca was the first to be a sun god in Aztec mythology. Maybe the Aztec people were on to something metaphorically; without darkness, there is no light, or out of the darkness came the light. Quetzalcoatl was the second sun god after knocking down Tezcatlipoca from the sky. In the mythology, they are brothers as the story goes, "Tezcatlipoca ruled the first Sun when giants inhabited the world. A fight between Tezcatlipoca and the god Quetzalcoatl, who wanted to replace him, put an end to this first world with the giants being devoured by jaguars." The next god to be chosen in the third creation story to be the Sun was Tlaloc, god of rain, lightning, and agriculture; as Carwright states, "Tláloc was associated with any meteorological conditions connected with water such as rain, clouds, storms, floods, lightning, snow, ice, and even droughts." I find it a bit of an oxymoron, the god of rain can also be the god of the Sun as well. The fourth sun god of the Aztecs, Chalchuihtilcue happened to be the consort of Tlaloc. According to the myth, "The fourth Sun (called Nahui Atl Tonatiuh or 4 Water) was ruled by Chalchiutlicue as a world of water, where fish species were marvelous and abundant. After 676 years, Chalchiutlicue destroyed the world in a cataclysmic flood, transforming all the humans into fish." (Maestri)

After four failed attempts to find a sun god worthy, the gods got together and decided the next sun god would have to sacrifice his/or her life by jumping into a fire kindled by the old fire god Huehueteotl, in order to become the god of the Sun this time. The Fifth and final sun god for the Aztec people became Nanahatzin, who jumped in the fire bravely and courageous and came out as the Sun to continue to shine on the earth. The Incan empire worshipped the sun god Inti, second only to the supreme deity Viracocha. Inca writings attribute him with the giver of life, controlling sunlight, warmth, and the agriculture of the earth. The people-built temples and pillars (to mark the solstices) in Cuzco, giving reverence to Inti, assisting them in the worship of the god. Inti was known as a benevolent god that was good to the people. Only when an eclipse appears, he is showing his wrath, and sacrifice must be made to appease, "The Inca could not predict solar eclipses, and when one occurred, it tended to trouble them greatly. The diviners would attempt to figure out why Inti was displeased, and sacrifices would be offered. The Inca rarely practiced human sacrifice, but an eclipse sometimes was considered cause to do so." (Minster)

In my brief survey, I noticed that the West's sun gods have similar backgrounds and attributes, which leads me to believe there was some admixture going on. It is not by coincidence they all have similar creation stories. Notice how sun gods of the west ride in chariots across the sky led by horses. The only variant is Ra is on a boat instead of a chariot, and this can be one of two things; the people of Kemet did not have chariots at the time, or Ra is just simply older. The question one should be asking, are boats older than chariots? The introduction of chariots in Kemet did come in after eleven dynastic periods by way of the Hyksos.

Part IV (As I Learn We All Learn)

SURVEY SEVEN

The Legend of 'Alī Ber Shī 'Alī Sunnī 'Alī (1464-92)

By: Ini-Herit Shawn P

When we travel through Bilād al-Sūdān historically, we tend to learn all the oral traditions of years past. We hear the djele tell us epic stories about the kings of the past and how they established a presence among others that drew the people to them for eternity. In Mali, the most spoken of and revered King was Sundiata, rightfully so his story is glorified among its people for what he was able to establish that allows his predecessors, more specifically his descendants, to build on his legacy greatness. And then there was Sonnī Alī, depending on which external source you are reading, he ruled with an iron fist that seems to leave an internal bruise that struck fear in those who crossed his path. How he would come to rule could be explained by a period of weakness and political mayhem. In this chapter, we will review two primary texts, specifically Ta'rīkh al-Sūdān and Ta'rīkh al-Fattāsh, among a few secondary and tertiary sources to properly understand just who Sonnī Alī was to his people and is historically. I believe that historians have intentionally misrepresented his reign due to how he ruled. He feared no man, and he ruled his way.

"On the death of Mūsā II, a succession crisis pitted the descendants of Sundiata against those of his younger brother, Mande Bory. Rulers were assassinated, and royal power was weakened. In the fifteenth century, the Tuareg finally conquered Timbuktu, Walāta, and Nema. This affected Mali's trans-Saharan relations. The emergence of Songhay under Sonnī 'Alī was a decisive setback both for the expansion of the Tuareg and for Malian hegemony, which was only given a second breath by trade with the Portuguese." (Ly-Tall 1997:1) Songhay faced political pressure from multiple sources for quite some time, especially after everyone wanted a piece of Mali's empire after the political move made during the reign of Mansā Mūsā on the grand stage in Cairo.

One problem I have with the fourteenth century in West Africa is the Coming of the Europeans, more specifically, the Portuguese. Anytime you have them trying to establish themselves near or around an area, it usually has everything to do with resources and slaves, so nothing good could ever come out of the presence of yet another foreign instigator in Bilād al-Sūdān. "The mid-ninth/fifteenth-century arrival of the Portuguese along the West African coast was not the principal reason for a reorientation of power in the region, as that process had actually begun at least fifty years prior.In the aftermath of Mansā Sulaymān's reign, Mali faltered due to succession disputes, in tandem with a central administrative apparatus challenged by a sprawling territorial expanse. Growing Malian weakness encouraged the rise of alternative political formations, and though Mali would continue well into the eleventh/seventeenth century, it would do so in diminished form, losing control over vital spaces of commercial and cultural exchange in both the Senegal and Niger valleys.

The Middle Niger is the focus of what follows, where dawned a polity that, though tethered to Malian antecedent in important ways, nonetheless forged a model of state power never witnessed there. The onset of Songhay was a reemergence in that it re-centered the ancient town of Gao, the capital of the novel experiment. Inheriting the mantle of Mali, Songhay would undertake important innovations in meeting the demands of international commerce, ethnic diversity, and Islam's expansion." (Gomez 2018:169) We began to see the ethnic diversity wage a wedge in the political, cultural, and community presence in Songhay. This speaks to the non-blacks infiltrating areas that once upon a time they could not establish. We can blame the conversion to Islam, and it's spread because it influenced the people. "Informed by both local practice and international engagement, Songhay would eventually achieve a remarkable social compact by which new levels of mutual respect and tolerance were reached and through which Songhay came to be characterized. In this way, it distinguished itself from its Malian predecessor, for - although inclusive of non-Mande elements - the Malian empire was first and foremost a Mande operation, in which the Mande sought to control all levers of political, social, and cultural power, something even Mansā Mūsā sought to consolidate through his indigenization program. In contrast, Songhay would evolve differently, becoming a much more ethnically heterogeneous society in which allegiance to the state transcended loyalties to clan and culture, with its leadership becoming much more diverse." (Gomez 2018:169-170)

Here lies the problem during the era of turmoil; this cultural assimilation and adaptation began to allow real acceptance of non-Malian and Mande elements, as Gomez stated, which led to this heterogenous nightmare that orchestrated the fall of a great Empire. When we observed history from a far and deal with the overall loss of our identity as a people, we are always looking for foreign acceptance. In that, we allow them to critique our way of life and infuse their cultural ideology unto us, and within that acceptance, we slowly began to lose who we are. Of course, this acculturation transpired for a few centuries. The presence of the early Muslim converts in pockets of the empire along trade routes which they oversaw in their own interaction of economic and political gain, and during the Islamic expansion, traditionalists served as prey for conversion, slaves, and examples that lead to many deaths. Now that the stage has been set to introduce the world to Sunni 'Alī we will now bear witness to the man, the myth, and the legend who would assume power under challenging times. We need to keep in mind that Sunni 'Alī was a traditionalist at heart who often mixed Islam with his ancestral beliefs. This did not sit well with some Muslims. "However, Sonni 'Alī was castigated in the local seventeenth-century chronicle the Ta'rikh al-Sūdān, for not being a good Muslim (Es-Sa'di

1900:103; Hunwick 1999), and was condemned for making sacrifices, consulting soothsayers, and for persecuting the Muslim scholars of Timbuktu." (Insoll 2003:255)

"Before the reign of Sunnī 'Alī (1464-1492), Songhai was just a small state on the Niger. In less than thirty years Sunnī 'Alī turned his small kingdom into a great Empire based on the River Niger, which served as its lifeline. In 1468 he took Timbuktu from the Tuareg, who had seized control of it forty years earlier. Four years later, in 1472, he took the important island city of Jenne on the River Bani, a tributary of the Niger. Jenne was famous not only as a commercial center but as a home of Muslim scholars. From Jenne, Sunni 'Alī went on to bring what remained of Mali under his control. In 1483 Sunni 'Alī decisively defeated the Mossi of Yatenga, who had been raiding his territory. However, though he managed to keep them out of Songhai, he could never make them tributary to him. In 1492, in the course of another expedition, he was killed. He left behind him the most powerful state in Western and Central Sūdān, comprising many different peoples." (Crowder 1977:48)

"The coming of Sunni 'Alī was an event of vast proportions and profound implications, occupying a status proximate to that of Sunjata himself. In parallel fashion, Sunni 'Alī was largely responsible for exponentially increasing the territorial reach of Songhay; in a real sense, the empire begins with him. And like Sunjata, he is intimately associated with war, emerging as a tireless warrior, the consummate general of his time, veritably transforming both physical and human landscapes through incessant campaigning. But unlike Sunjata, he is also recognized for establishing political control over leading commercial entrepôts, in particular Timbuktu and Jenne, and doing so in a manner strikingly different from the efforts of Mansā Mūsā. And unlike Sunjata or Mūsā, he acquired quite the reputation, notorious as well as controversial, for his treatment of Muslim elites. Sunni 'Alī's imperial policies and their relation to religious communities would long animate the decision-making process in imperial Songhay." (Gomez 2018:183) Based on the accounts of Crowder and Gomez, one would assume that Sunni 'Alī seems to rule in a way that brought him national attention, glory, and a physical presence at times turmoil had reshaped the landscape and cultural influence among true Mande people. However, you had some who saw him as nothing more than an evildoer.

According to Hunwick when Songhay is mentioned, he states, "Inevitably we must begin with the reign of Sunni 'Alī (1464-92), for it was under his energetic and imperial spirit that Songhay was transformed from a relatively small homogenous state into a large multi-ethnic empire. 'Ali-Bēr, as he was also known, was the last effective ruler who bore the title Sunni or Shi (probably more correctly Sõnyī), inherited from the days of 'Alī Golom, the Mali commander, and son of a Songhay ruler, who wrested his homelands from the suzerainty of Mali in the late thirteenth century. Although his predecessor, Salmān Dāma (or Dandi), had devastated Mama, a province of northern Mali, it was not integrated into Songhay proper. The Ta'rikh al-Sūdān is explicit: 'The sovereignty of none of them (the Sunnis) extended beyond 'Songhay' except for Sunni 'Alī.'' (Ajaye & Crowder 1972:225) Hunwick seems to take a more balanced approach calling him the last effective ruler regardless of his method; the way he ruled his empire indeed was just that a success due to expansion and control. However, we will now look into the Ta'rikhs and get an overall perspective of just who Sunni 'Alī was during his reign.

"The successor of Simān-Dāma was the tyrant, the debauched, the cursed, the oppressor, the Shī 'Alī, the last king of this dynasty, who was a model of shameful conduct for his entourage. The Shī 'Alī was always victorious, pillaging every land on which he fixed his choice. Whenever he was present, his armies were never defeated or vanquished: they were always victorious. From Santa to Sibiridugu, his horses ran over all these lands, where he made war on his own people. The meaning of this word shī is given in a text I saw that was written by the hand of Mahmūd, one of our imams: 'The meaning of shī,' he states, 'is Koi-banandi; in other words, the caliph of the sultan, his deputy or replacement.' The Shī 'Alī was a tyrannical king. His heart was so hard that he once threw a baby into a mortar and forced the mother to grind it, even while the baby was still alive. The flesh was then fed to his horses. He was debauched and impious; in fact, one of the shykhs of his time, who lived at Mōri-Koira, was asked if those of an infidel though he made the profession of faith twice-over and spoke as a man who was well-versed in the teachings of Islam." (Kati,Wise 2011:87-88) The Fattāsh immediately refuses to hold back in one sense Mahmūd Kati expressing displeasure with Shī 'Alī and then in the same sense; he acknowledges the shī's success during his reign. Mahmūd Kati did not hesitate to bring up the incident regarding the baby and its mother as to defame the character of the shī. Regardless of his success, this man was a baby killer who once made a mother grind her child into meat and feed it to horses. Now I would be doing you an injustice if I do not mention this. I have not been able to cross-reference that claim successfully; therefore, relying on external sources has provided us some limitations regarding Kati's claim. However, he said what he said, and if it appears in other places, it's based on his words.

"As for the great oppressor and notorious evil-doer, Sunni 'Alī (Sunni spelt with an undated sīn accompanied by a gamma and a doubled nūn with kasra - thus I found it in the Dhayl al-dībāj of the erudite scholar, the jurist Ahmad Bābā - may God Most High have mercy on him).

He was a man of great strength and colossal energy, a tyrant, a miscreant, an aggressor, a despot (mutasallit), and a butcher who killed so many human beings that only God Most High could count them. He tyrannized the scholars and holy men, killing them, insulting them, and humiliating them. The erudite scholar and hāfiz al-'Alqamī - may God

Most High have mercy on him - in his commentary on al-Jāmi' al-saghīr of al-Suyūtī said, in reference to the notable events of the ninth century: 'Alī who destroyed both lands and people. He came to power in 869/1464-5'. It is related to the authority of the Friend of God Most High, the jurist, Qāḍī Abū 'l-Barakāt Maḥmūd b. 'Umar b. Muḥammad Aqīt, that his own date of birth preceded Sunni 'Alī's accession by one year, and I saw in the Kitāb al-dhayl [the statement]: '[Qāḍī Maḥmūd] was born - may God Most High have mercy on him - in the year 868/1463-4, and died in the year 955, on Friday night 16 Ramaḍān/18 Oct. 1548.' End of quotation. Sunni 'Alī remained in power either twenty-seven or twenty-eight years." (Hunwick 203:91)

In the Ta'rikh al-Sūdān we see similar gratitude and displeasure paid toward 'Alī Bēr it seems as if his bad outweighed his goods regardless of his expansions of the Empire. We know that Arabs hated the way he tormented the scholars of Timbuktu and that never sat well nor did the way he invaded with his military in areas where Islamic presence was already dominant. However, it's simply more to the story that meets the eyes regarding Shī 'Alī.

"Let some of his most impious acts be known: this man would put jurists to death! He destroyed villages, burning the inhabitants in the flames! He inflicted all sorts of tortures on people. Sometimes he would light the fires to kill them. Sometimes he immured his victims, leaving them to die while still alive, and sometimes he would cut open the womb of a living woman and rip out her fetus! In the end, his acts of cruelty and those who served under him were so numerous that it would be impossible to record them all in a single volume. He besieged the kingdom of the Songhay in the year 69 of the ninth century [September 3, 1464 - August 23, 1465], holding onto power for twenty-seven years, four months, and fifteen days, until the year 807 [November 4, 1491 - October 22, 1492]. I learned this from the work entitled Durar al-hisān fi Akbar bad mulūk al-sūdān. The author of this work is Bābā Goro ion al-hajj Muhammad bin al-hajj al-Amīn Gano. The Shī 'Alī had no enemies he hated as much as the Fulani. He could not look at a Fulani without killing them, even if they were under the protection of a family that was not Fulani. He accepted no Fulani councilors or magistrates in his cabinet. He decimated the tribe of the Sangare, leaving a small fraction of these people alive, a fraction so tiny that they could all be hidden in the shadow of a single tree. He enslaved Muslims of free condition and presented them as gifts to other Muslims, pretending to be generous in doing so." (Kati/Wise 2011:88-89) Kati has so much hatred in his expressions about the person 'Alī was that he wanted to make sure to list every detail as possible so that people would not revere Shī 'Alī in any way that would validate him as a true ruler of his era.

Part of the problem is the fact Sunni 'Alī enslaved other Muslims and did not fully accept Islam. "According to the Ta'rikh al-Fattāsh Muhammad challenged Sunni Bāru to declare himself a Muslim and Sunni Bāru 'refused absolutely; he had fears for his sovereignty as is natural on the part of a ruler.' This statement highlights the struggle between Islam and indigenous cults as the elan vital of Songhay sovereignty." (Ajaye/Crowder 1972:227) Also, his behavior toward Fulani and the Taureg who controlled Timbuktu who often did business with the Portuguese Jews in the area. Sunni 'Alī military prowess was on overdrive during his reign; he conquered territories in Jenne, Jinjo, Bara, even Sanhāja Nono, but most notably is as mentioned before, his behavior and attitude toward as he entered Timbuktu. "Sunni 'Alī entered Timbuktu on 4 or 5 Rajab 873/18 or 19 Jan. 1469, in the fourth or fifth year of his reign. He perpetrated terrible wickedness in the city, putting it to flame, sacking it, and killing large numbers of people.

When Akil heard of his approach, he assembled a thousand camels and mounted the scholars of Timbuktu and took them to Bīru, declaring that their fate was of paramount importance to him. Among them was the faqīh 'Umar b. Muhammad Aqīt and his three divinely favored sons, the faqīh 'Abd Allāh, the faqīh Ahmad, who was the eldest of them, and the faqīh Mahmūd, who was the youngest, being only five years old at the time and unable to ride a camel or walk [such a distance]. The only solution was for him to be put on the shoulders of their slave, Jiddu Makkankī, who carried him there. Among others who went was the maternal uncle of these three, al-Mukhtār al-Nahwī, son of the jurist [Qādi] Anda Ag-Muhammad. In Bīru he found Imam al-Zammūri - may God Most High have mercy on him - who gave him an ijāza for the Kitāb al-shifā of Qādi 'Iyād - may

God Most High have mercy on him. On the day they left Timbuktu, you could see grown men with beards anxious to mount a camel but trembling in fear before it. When they mounted the camel, they were thrown off when the beast rose, for the righteous forefathers used to keep their children indoors until they grew up. Hence, they had no understanding of practical matters since they did not play in their youth, and play makes a child smart and gives him insight into many things. Their plight caused them to regret this, and after they returned to Timbuktu, they allowed their children to play and released them from their confinement. The evil oppressor [Sunni 'Alī] set about killing or humiliating those scholars who remained in Timbuktu for their alleged friendship with the Tuareg and membership in their elite, for which reason he hated them. He imprisoned Sita bt. Anda Ag-Muhammad, the mother of the jurist Mahmūd, and put her two brothers, the jurists Mahmūd and Ahmad, to death. He heaped continuous insults and humiliations on the scholars - may God spare us from that. One day when he was at the port of Kabara he ordered that thirty virgin daughters of theirs be brought for him to take as concubines and gave orders that they must come on foot. They set off never before having emerged from the seclusion of their homes. When they reached a certain point, they were completely unable to go any further, so the official whom Sunni 'Alī had sent to conduct them to him sent him word of this. Sunni 'Alī ordered that they should be put to death, and they all were - may God spare us from such things. The place where this happened was near the western side of

Amadia and is called Finā radar al-abkār - 'the arena of virgins' fate." (Hunwick 2011:93-94)

'Alī would continue humiliating and killing scholars of Timbuktu and those who fled he captured them in other towns bringing them to their death right where they stood. Those he did not kill, he imprisoned it and did not matter if it was a woman or a man whatever he saw fit at that time he meant it. Shī 'Alī didn't care about the stature or worthiness of the people who fled; he was on a mission to terrorize whoever stood in his path. There was an incident where Sunni 'Alī made someone stand in the sun all day long and tortured them. However, despite the way he treated those scholars, he did acknowledge their worth. "He would say, 'Were it not for the scholars, life would not be pleasant or agreeable. (Hunwick 2011:95)

It has been said that he acted the way he did on his path of destruction only to make a mockery of his faith. He would worship totally different that than those around him and pick and choose when to pray. "Ali had no use for Islam, the religion of urban communities. Its learned men constituted a state within a state and were critical of rulers for lukewarmness in Islam and indulgence in pagan rites. Confident in his own power, 'Ali did not need their support and refused to compromise with a religion which involved paying allegiance to a law higher than himself." (Saad 1983:42) He would also order a person to be killed; it did not matter how close the person was to him. But people did not kill who he ordered; they would hide them away and wait to see if he repented and then inform him that they had spared that person's life and would be grateful for that. It is said that this often happened with Askiya Muhammad, who was his official during his reign. He threatened everyone aunts, uncles, cousins, children, neighbors, whoever. It did not matter to him if he felt a need to disrespect someone; he did it with no ill will. If he was not a war with everyone, he demonstrated his dominance over someone inferior to him. "The ferocity of the Shī 'Alī towards Muslims and his cruelty in all worldly things, as well as in matters of religion, made the hearts of the people overflow with sadness and worry. Deliverance seemed beyond hope, for his reign had lasted so many years that it seemed as if these curses would never cease." (Katie/Wise 2011:101)

"The account of Sunni 'Alī reign in Ta'rīkh al-Fattāsh is heavily skewed toward summaries of military itineraries, conquests, and territorial expansion, subjects that either receive short shrift or are contextualized differently in Ta'rīkh al-Sūdān. To be sure, Ta'rīkh al-Fattāsh criticizes Sunni 'Alī's war conduct, specifically his cruelty, and subjects his general character to a generous sprinkling of opprobrium, but what emerges most saliently is the recognition, if not celebration, or imperialism that equates with greatness and glory. For, in the final analysis, Sunni 'Alī was also 'Alī Her, 'Alī 'the Great,' with Ta'rīkh al-Fattāsh as a principal witness. The trope of conquest actually begins with Sunni 'Alī's predecessors, for which there are two independent traditions. The first concert one Mādao (alternatively, Māda'o, Muhammad Dao, Muhammad Dā'o, Muhammad Dā'u), the father of Sunni 'Alī. According to the Ta'rīkh al-Fattāsh's manuscript C, Mādao was responsible for the defeat of the Malian emperor, after which they took possession of the controversial twenty-four tribes. However, the dubious placement of Shehu Amadu Lobbo's thirteenth/nineteenth-century claim to these groups within a transfer of authority between Mali and Songhay some five hundred years prior does not eviscerate the notion that imperial impulses began with Mādao. The second tradition of Songhay imperialism is associated with Sulaymān (Sulīman) Dāma, otherwise known as 'Dandi,' credited with an assault on the 'irresistible power of Mema. Ta'rīkh al-Fattāsh states Mema province had broken away from Mali, a further indication of Mali's weakening condition. Sunni Sulaymān Dāma sacked the land of Mema, 'annihilating them and destroying their power." (Gomez 2018:183-84)

Any expansion of an empire will lead to bloodshed, especially under current unsettled situations such as those Shī 'Alī faced. In the face of a foreign control over Timbuktu and an emerging presence of Portuguese traders, missionaries, and enslavers, one could rightfully state a tyrant was needed at that time. Based on the external perspectives of Shī 'Alī only Arab Muslims seem to be bothered by the way he governed and ruled due to the fact he attacked scholars at Timbuktu, didn't really much care for the Tuareg, and wouldn't conform to Islam the way that they wanted him to. However, his death is one of many mysteries and conspiracies. Could the end of his reign come at the hands of his own or a foreigner from a distant land? Either way, his transition can be seen as a gift and a curse in the history of Songhay.

The Death of Shī 'Alī (Alī Bēr) Sunni 'Alī

"This dispute between the pure Muslim and the mixer is very important in the history of West Africa. The pure Muslim says that you shall worship no other god but Allah, whatever the circumstances. If you do worship other gods, you are not a Muslim but a pagan, and it is legitimate for the pure Muslim to wage jihad or Holy war against you. Many kings in West African history, however, while they became Muslim, felt that to keep the loyalty of all their subjects, Muslims and non-Muslims alike, they had to maintain their role as head of the traditional religions of their states." (Crowder 1977:49) Could this be the reason behind the death of Shī 'Alī because he refused to conform, and he was totally against conforming to the point he even mocked being a Muslim which in all honesty disrespected the beliefs of pure Muslims. He relied more on the traditional beliefs of his mother versus foreign romanticists. Or was it his idol threats he threw around when he got bored when he would order his men to kill certain people close to him? Maybe it was someone seeking revenge for the death of their people and land due to Shī 'Alī's behavior as an aggressive general who had an undying motor for wreaking havoc on those who stood in his way. Did he fall in a military campaign against the Tuareg, whom he was trying hard to defeat? Or did he die by drowning, which is mentioned in the Ta'rikh al-Sūdān?

"In 894/1488 Modibbo Zunkāki died, {71} while in 898/1492 Sunni 'Alī, son of Muhammad Dao, himself died as he returned from a campaign in Gurma, where he had fought the Joghorani and the Fulani. While en route back through Gurma, a torrent overtook him at a place called Kuna, bringing about his death through the Mighty and Powerful One agency. This occurred on 15 Muharram 898/6 Nov. 1492. They say that his son removed his entrails and filled his abdomen with honey to prevent it from stinking - may God Most High make that a requital for what he did to people in his lifetime during the days of his tyranny. Then his army encamped at Ba'anyiya." (Hunwick 2003:100-01) It is said that a flood had claimed his life, but oral traditions tell another story about the death of Shī 'Alī. "Oral tradition, on the other hand, asserts that he was killed by Mamar, a son of his sister Kassey (and later to be askia al-hajj Muhammad I), who was at the time, according to Arabic sources, Tondi-farima, or 'governor of the rock' (the Hombori/Bandiagara regions). No less mysterious is the origin of Muhammad himself." (Ajaye/Crowder 1972:227). Another source Cissoko substantiates that claim: "The last Sonnī, rejecting Islam, was driven from power by the Hombori-Koy Toure or Sylla, a convinced Muslim, who created the dynastic title of askiya." (Kerbo/Niane 1997:79)

The Ta'rikh al-Fattāsh takes a different route in pursuit of the death of Shī 'Alī and says, "The ferocity of the Shī 'Alī towards Muslims and his cruelty in all worldly things, as well as in matters of religion, made the hearts of the people overflow with sadness and worry. Deliverance seemed beyond hope, for his reign had lasted so many years that it seemed as if these curses would never cease. However, the day of deliverance came at last, thanks to an impoverished holy man, whose daughter had been raped by the shī. When this unfortunate man came to complain at the prince's home, the shī swore that he would cast him into the fires if he did not depart from his presence at once. The man left with tears in his eyes; then, raising his hands to the heavens and turning on the path towards Mecca, he cried out: 'Oh my God! Oh, Master! You who are near us! You who are the ruler of all things! You who see, know, and hear all. I humbly beg you to crush this lustful and lewd creature. I implore You to break this perverse man, who has profited for so long from Your indifference, who, deluded by Your inaction, dares to trample upon a man of God! Hear my prayer and come to my aid! I beg You.' This very day the shī was visited by two holy men who were descended from the Mōri Hawgāru, ancestor of the people of Mōri-Koira. One of them was named the Mōri al-Sādiq, and the other was named the Mōri Jeiba. They came to lodge a complaint of mistreatment against someone in his family; that is to say, the family of the Shī 'Alī. When he saw these two men, the Shī 'Alī ordered that they be seized at once, placed in chains, and then conducted to an island and left to die: 'Oh my God,' cried one of them. 'Protect us from this man! Make him perish this very instant!' - The other man then cried out, 'And see that he perishes in a state of infidelity, not in a state of belief in Islam!' At this very instant, the shī, who was staying at a settlement in the land of al-Hajar that was named Donna was unexpectedly struck dead by God." (Kati/Wise 2011:101-02)

The Fattāsh hints at infidelity by the Shī and his inability to address the father's concerns who came to file his complaint about the mishandling of his daughter, and the Shī just dismisses. Also, a cause of concern yet again was his belief in Islam and how he did not take it seriously, making him susceptible to being overthrown. However, the Fattāsh agrees with the Sūdān regarding him drowning or being struck down by God as it states, but it was the rapids at Koni after his march on the Fulani that settled his faith. Another assertion based on oral history was that Askia Muhammad set him up. One could conclude that all those death threats thrown at him by Shī would provoke him to retaliate against 'Alī, which would help provoke a clean break from traditional practices. Gomez poses a clearer perspective qualifying the external sources, oral traditions, and the political threat that posed a threat to Shī 'Alī's rule.

Alī could have been concerned that the return of Muhammad Aqīt's eldest son, preceded by that of his brother Mahmūd and uncle al-Mukhtār al-Nahwī, signaled an attempt to reestablish their influence, and even that of the Tuareg, an interpretation strengthens by the assertion that Muhammad Aqīt himself once entertained designs on the city (to be examined). If he was a threat before making hājj as well as the prestige of having met such Egyptian notables as Jalāl al-Dīn 'Abd al-Rahmān b. Abī Bakr al-Suyūti (d. 905/1505) and grammarian Khālid b. 'Abd Allāh b. Abī Bakr al-Azharī (d. 905/1499). Such would be Ahmad b. 'Umar's renown that he would become a celebrated teacher, circulating as far as Kano while amassing some seven hundred columns in his personal library. If his return in fact, alarmed the Sunni, the latter's response would anticipate that of the Moroccan Pasha Mahmūd b. Zarqūn, one hundred years later, who also suspected the Aqīts of fomenting unrest in close association with the Tuareg. The imprisonment of the Timbuktu-koi, whether or not connected to Ahmad, nonetheless coincided with the beginning of a purge that would (again) target the Aqīts. Those departing for Hawki would include Ahmad b. 'Umar and his brother Mahmūd, the latter's accord with the Sunni apparently undone." (Gomez 2018:206)

So political pressure from an uncle with hopes of restoring the presence of the Tuareg, undoing all the work Shī 'Alī did by expanding the empire, removing the ancestral ways of old, and to add dethroning Shī from his seat would not go over well without a fight. Gomez continues: "Five years following this fifth purge, Sunni 'Alī was dead. The sources do not address what transpired between Gao, Timbuktu, and Hawki in those years. Still, circumstantial evidence indicates a high level of tension between an elite, targeted scholarly community and Songhay's head of state. Matters were at an impasse, and though a coup d'erat cannot be unequivocally demonstrated, the necessary elements were coming together.

If encouraged by the scholars, military capability would be required." (Gomez 2018:206)

This proves to be accurate based on how Sunnī 'Alī met his fate in what was supposed to have been a drowning due to a flood, but reading multiple accounts reveals he died alone while his army was unharmed. This plot settled in secrecy between high-level ranking members of 'Alī's military and as the oral traditions state: "Indeed, the oral traditions are emphatic in accusing the Tondi-farma of assassinating Sunnī 'Alī, while Kasay's promise that in return for Nānā Tinti's intercessory prayers her son Muhammad Sure would 'make you rejoice in your children and relatives' assumes a tangible quality, as the al-Hājj and Aqīt families were the major beneficiaries of Muhammad Ture's emergence. 'When Askia Muhammad acceded to power,' Ta'rīkh al-Sūdān remarks, 'he kept this promise.' This comes will nigh to acknowledging a prior conspiracy." (Gomez 2018:207)

The fate of Sunnī 'Alī son was at the hands of a man he's threatened the life of on several occasions. Not only the life of that person but his family's name al-Hājj, who he continuously tormented. "We have it on record that Sunni 'Ali humiliated several members of the al-Hājj family and on one occasion caused al-Faqīh Ibrāhīm, son of Abu Bakr, to stand a whole day under the scorching sun as a humiliation and punishment. Subsequently, certain members of the apparently large clan fled to Tagedda to seek Tuareg support on a large scale. The Songhai commander retaliated by killing many of those remaining and imprisoning others, both men and women, and a party fled towards Walāta was overtaken at Shīb and massacred to the man. We do not know when precisely this happened, but stories of the martyrs became powerful legends among Tuaregs in the east where members of the al-Ḥājj clan settled permanently." (Saad 1983:44) However, the military even honored the move by remaining silent regarding the plot and carried out the death as a natural death caused by a flood that didn't happen. To be more accurate, the time of Shī 'Alī's death appears to have been during the dry seasons; however, there were two lakes nearby. Some say he threw himself into the lake and drowned, but some assume he was drowned by the man who would usurp his son after his death and come to rule longer than any of his predecessors have in history.

> "Even in his own lifetime, Sunni 'Ali approached an image comparable to that of an Antichrist in the minds of devout Muslims. The Egyptian scholar al-Suyūti, though he never visited the Sūdān, described his rise to power as a calamity comparable to the loss of Spanish lands by Islam." - Saad 1983:45

SURVEY EIGHT

Page 145

Morocco, Ahmad al-Mansur & The Demise of Songhai

By: Sutekh Akande Iyanu-Oluwa

As one of the greatest empires in West African history but one of the prominent superpowers of world history, the Songhai empire is revered in African-centered circles worldwide. With some of the most legendary champions and warriors of the African continent, it is shocking to see how hastily this entity declined. As African advocates we may sometimes be guilty of emphasizing the high points of African histories, while shying away from the less favorable elements. As a student of history, I feel it necessary to view these historical issues as an enlightening revelation. No powerful world entity is without its complications. This includes Morocco as well. In this chapter, we will take a journey back in time to the brink of the early modern era to conclude some of the factors that played a role in the Moroccan invasion and ultimate downfall of the Songhai empire, to hopefully take away valuable lessons that may be used for the cohesiveness and "progress" of an African continental and diasporic peoples. I pose that the advantage of technological advancement.

Abu ʿĀmir Muḥammad ibn ʿAbdullāh ibn Abi ʿĀmir al-Maʿafiri is a man that would today be known by a simple moniker, al-Mansur ("He who is victorious"). Coming into the power of the Moroccan throne at about 30 years old, he was a towering, tall man with full cheeks, dark black hair and dark eyes, extremely white teeth & golden-brown skin complexion (Garcia-Arenal, 2009, pg. 32). The title of al-Mansur was not always a nickname of his. This illustrious epithet was given to him after he was the ruling survivor in the Battle of Alcazar, affectionately known as "The Battle of 3 Kings". Succeeding this battle, he became victorious (Hamel, 2013, pg. 145).

One of the central issues to Morocco having such a massive advantage over the populous warriors of the conglomerate that was the Songhai Empire was ballistics. Guns were a part of the Moroccan army. A "Barbary Company" was started thanks to a partnership with England in 1585 via a British merchant. Al-Mansur was linked with Queen Elizabeth I of England through this affiliation. The British traded firearms in return for saltpeter, mainly used as a preservative for food, among other uses (Hamel, 2013, pg. 146).

The arquebus (matchlock muskets) were the guns of the day. The arquebus was invented in the 15th century. Burning hemp or rope made from cotton was saturated in saltpeter at the uppermost part of the serpentine. The container holding the gunpowder was joined by the "match," which was on the upper serpentine, by pulling on the lower part of the serpentine. The matchlock arquebus was, at the time, the firearm most used in combat. Usually, they were about 5-6 feet long and were used with a rest stand for the barrel when firing (Conrad, 2005, pg. 63). This technological advancement would become an essential variable in the decisiveness of the Songhai empire collapse. The Sorko people, fishers, and river specialists were among the first groups in the Gao area via small settlements on the Niger riverbank. After the Sorko, came the Gow group, the hunters, and then Do/Doh people, who are the farmers. Before the 10th century, these groups of people were subjugated by a Songhai-speaking group who utilized horses. They all gradually began to speak the same language and collectively became known as the Songhai (Conrad, 2005, pg. 49). Eventually, Songhai replaced the Mali empire as the most powerful entity in the region and began to undergo large territorial expansion (Holst, 2016, pg. 60).

The first notable dynasty of the Songhai was the Sunni dynasty, with one of the most renowned rulers and warriors of the modern era, Sunni Ali Ber, who came to power in 1464, and his reign lasted until 1492 (Williams, 1971, pg. 204). The next dynasty to rule the Songhai would be the Askiya dynasty, headed by the most famous king of this "house," Askiya al-Hajj Muhammad Ture. Affectionately known as Askiya the Great, he deposed Sunni Baru, the successor of Sunni Ali, and usurped the throne (Hunwick, 2003, pg. 103). This is the dynasty that began a lot of the succession quarrels, which was another factor in the downfall of the Songhai. Next to rule was Askiya Muhammad's son, Askiya Musa, who overthrown his father and was murdered by his oppositional brothers. Then came Askiya Muhammad Bonkana. He took power from Alu, son of Askiya al-Hajj Muhammad Ture, who opposed him. He was overthrown by Dendi-Fari – the highest-ranking military captain in the empire. Another son of Askiya the Great, Askiya Ishma'il, was appointed by the same Dendi-Fari that deposed Askiya Muhammad Bonkana and Ishma'il later died in Gao during his brother's military advances. Askiya Ishaq I, another son of Askiya the Great, was appointed the new Askiya by his brothers when they made it back to Gao to find that Ishma'il was deceased. Ishaq was a cold-hearted brutal murderer to anyone that he perceived as a threat to his position as ruler of the throne to Songhai. He is also famously noted for defending his right to the Tagaza salt mines from Muhammad al-Arak, sultan of Morocco. Ishaq died in Kukiya of natural causes. Ishaq's successor was Askiya Dawud, a brother of his. Dawud apparently had no one to ever oppose his rule (Hunwick, 2003, pg. 336-337).

Askiya Dawud was a powerful king who was spoken very highly of – feared by the opposition but respected and very loved by his subjects. Dawud is perceived by many to be the 3rd great ruler of the nation of Songhai. First was Sunni Ali, then Askiya the Great, and now Askiya Dawud. The nation was taken to new heights under his command. David C. Conrad details a way in which Dawud revolutionized the accession to the royal seat: "Up to this time, all of the askiyas had been sons of Muhammad, except for the usurper Muhammad Bonkana, a nephew. Many other sons of Askiya Muhammad had held high offices and titles. During the 34-year reign of Askiya Dawud, as these important offices became vacant, he usually appointed his own sons to the positions. Thus, Askiya Dawud gradually eliminated from high office the offspring of other sons of Askiya Muhammad. From Askiya Dawud's time forward, all the askiyas were his descendants." (2005, pg. 59) The Askiya was victorious over most of his military campaigns, excluding a 1557 dispute over the Taghaza salt mines with Muhammad al-Shaykh – father of Ahmad al-Mansur and the Moroccan sultan of that time (Conrad, 2005, pg. 59).

Taghaza was a focal point of several conflicts between north Africa and the Bilad es Sudan (Land of the Blacks). The salt quarries of Taghaza were a big root of riches for the rulers of Bilad es Sudan. The 16th century was a time of struggle between Morocco and Songhai for these mines. They were also essential to the health of those in the region of the Sahara and their cattle. Ahmad al-Mansur sent soldiers to control the oases in Tuwat and Tigurarin areas. This necessitated the soldiers to take a long, risky journey into the heart of the Sahara. This would serve as a test to gauge if the soldiers could survive the harsh and dangerous climate and landscape. Al-Mansur's later scribe said that he had intentions of raiding the Sudan since this expedition (Garcia-Arenal, 2009, pg. 100-101).

The following year, in 1582, Askiya Dawud would perish of natural causes in his Tondibi residence (Hunwick, 2003, pg. 337). After his death, Songhai had an outbreak of quarrels over who will succeed to the seat of the throne. Ultimately, it was Askiya Muhammad al-Hajj. He was a Songhai ruler that never had a military crusade. This is due to the lower half of his body being afflicted by an illness. Also, he never participated in attacking or murdering his own brothers. But yet and still, his brothers replaced him, four years later, for Muhammad Bani because of their impatience, and Muhammad al-Hajj would soon die afterward (Conrad, 2005, pg. 59). The fratricide continued when Muhammad Bani. After rising to power, he immediately killed two of his brothers and buried them side by side (Hunwick, 2003, pg. 168). "He seems to have been the choice of those brothers who revolted against Askiya Al-Hajj, though others opposed him. He died, perhaps from an epileptic seizure, while waiting to engage Balmaca al-Sadiq in battle." (Hunwick, 2003, pg. 337)

The apex of the Songhai/Moroccan clash happens under the rule of Askiya Ishaq II, son of Askiya Dawud, who would be next in line in 1588. Muhammad Sadiq was an immediate problem because he wanted to overthrow Ishaq II with his army and loyal supporters that he had amassed. Somehow, Ishaq learned of a celebration in honor of Muhammad Saqid at Timbuktu and felt this was the perfect moment to strike. Ishaq's army of Gao and Sadiq's army of Timbuktu clashed in battle, with the Askiya becoming victorious in the end. Muhammad Sadiq had lost, and all Songhai warriors and officers that sided with him were captured and slain. So many died, on both sides, that the hole that it created in the Songhai military left them more vulnerable to an attack.

Commanders were replaced, but the mass of troops could not be restored (Conrad, 2005, pg. 61).

That same year, al-Mansur wrote to Ishaq II with a demand of 1 mithqal (3.64 grams) of gold for every load of salt from the salt mines of Taghaza while claiming the tax would fund armies of Islam to fight off "infidels" take back the land of al-Andalus. Before he penned this letter, he conferred with the ulama, who advised him that utilizing the salt mines without Imam authorization was legally immoral from an Islamic perspective.

Askiya Ishaq II rejected the notion of bowing down to the Moroccans in the fashion of recognizing the authority of al-Mansur as caliph and paying the gold tax proposed to him by the Sultan of Morocco. When news of this refusal reached the Sultan, he gathered his courtiers and ulama and divulged his plan to attack the Blacks of Songhai. He portrayed his invasion as a way to unify all Islamic forces under one command – his command – and take back lands that were lost. While Mansur thought that the Blacks could add physical and financial strength, he made clear that the Blacks could never become Imams because they were not of the Quraysh tribe, which is the tribe of the prophet Muhammad of Islam. The ulama disagreed with this decision because it was against sharia, Islamic law, to attack a Sunni nation that showed no antagonism or hostility towards Morocco. Also, they disagreed because of the difficulties of the journey through the Sahara. There was no precedence for this and no way to legalize it. (Garcia-Arenal, 2009, pg. 102)

Ahmad al-Mansur contended that the Blacks continued to fight with spears, lances, swords, and bows & arrows. In due course, he won over the ulama and broke down their resistance. Foreigners in Morocco at the time proposed that the idea of a campaign being funded by gold to take back Andalusia from the European Christians and Algiers from the Ottoman Turks may have its origins in with the Moriscos in the Sultan's army because this would appeal most to them (Garcia-Arenal, 2009, pg. 103).

Abd' al-Rahman al-Sa'di wrote that in 1589, Wuld Kirinfil, a slave of the royal court of Songhai, got on the wrong side of Askiya Ishaq II and was sent to Taghaza, which was under Songhai rule at the time, to be incarcerated.

Fig. 1: Soldier firing an Arquebus

Somehow Wuld broke away and escaped to Marrakesh, home of the Sadian Dynasty of Morocco. Wuld ran right into the protection of the Moroccans. He shared valuable information about the disorganization and the chaotic state that Songhai was in and encouraged the invasion of the disrupted empire via a letter directed to al-Mansur. Abd al-Aziz al-Fishtali, an official scribe of al-Mansur, posited that Wuld was actually a prince named Ali – Son of Dawud and brother of Ishaq, who was deposed. The more likely event is that Wuld lied about being a prince to give his message to the Sultaan more weight (Hamel, 2013, pg. 146-7).

Fig. 2: Map of Songhai's span at its peak

The Moroccan army set out for Songhai, in hopes of conquest and finding a new El Dorado, a root of precious gold, as they left Marrakesh in October of 1590. This was a small-scale but well-skilled force of 2,000 harquebusiers, half Moriscos and half renegades from Grenada, 500 mounted harquebusiers, and 1,500 lancers from Arab tribes. Convoys carrying supplies like food, water, ammo, ten mortars, four small cannons, tents, lots of gunpowder & material to siege walls accompanied the army. They used compasses to guide them through the dangerous desert, which was a 35-day trek. This journey had its consequences as many soldiers died of heatstroke or dehydration before reaching the destination of the river Niger. The expedition wore out the army, so instead of heading straight to Timbuktu; they went to the main place of opposition to Askiya Ishaq II – Gao (Garcia-Arenal, 2009, pg. 103-4). The man in control of this Moroccan military force was a blue-eyed, short Morisco eunuch, who was captured and castrated by Muslim slave raiders as a young boy – Jawdar Pasha (Hunwick, 2003, pg. 186) (Bovill, 1958, pg. 167).

At the back end of 1590, the Askiya got word about the approaching Moroccan army. Equipped with new commanders, Ishaq and his militia couldn't agree on a sound strategic plan; therefore, there was a lack of proper preparation on the part of Songhai. The commanders of the Askia posed a plan of sending soldiers to fill the wells in the desert to deny the Moroccan invaders of water. Ishaq was sent to ask the Tuareg to handle the task of the wells, but this attempt failed due to the attacking of the messengers by thieves. Moroccan soldiers spotted these wounded messengers with the letters from the Songhai ruler about filling the wells. Due to the Askiya's inability to make a move on Jawdar and his men in a sufficient timeframe, they had about two weeks to recover from their risky trans-Saharan trip to the Sudan (Conrad, 2005, pg. 61-2).

Finally, the historic battle took place at Tondibi, a land of cattle pasture north of Gao, on February 13, 1591. Askiya Ishaq II had a relatively large army complete with bows & arrows, soldiers mounted on horseback with lances and spears. The Songhai elite equaled about 8,000 with armbands made of gold. In addition, Songhai had oxen surrounding their forces to form a type of mobile wall in hopes of using them as a shield against the gunfire to allow Songhai warriors to get close enough to the enemy to engage in hand-to-hand combat (Garcia-Arenal, 2009, pg.105). Because of the firearms, Morocco had the upper hand in terms of warfare. Mulay Ahmad al-Mansur was fully aware that firearms were foreign to the Sudanese: "Among the reasons which prompted al-Mansûr to attack the Sudan, there was the fact that he had a number of cannons, mortars, rifles, and powder, from Christian territories, all things that were not in Morocco before him and had neither reached nor known in Sudan. The advisers bowed.". For the Blacks, long-range weapons were seen as cowardly and a blemish on one's honor (Holst, 2016, pg. 65-6).

The swords and spears of the defending Songhai proved to be no match for the advanced warfare technology of the Saadian military forces, even with numbers much fewer than that of Songhai. The oxen wall, meant to provide cover as Songhai troops approached the Moroccans for close combat, was a plan that backfired. As shots rang out from the European ballistics, the oxen were so confused and chaotic that they, instead, charged the Songhai warriors themselves. The elite of the Songhai dropped their shields to the ground, all kneeling while tying their foot to their thigh. This pose was taken as they fired arrows from their immobilized position to show that they had no intent on withdrawal. This was said to be a courageous act to push the remaining army members to fight with greater vigor. Projectiles from Moroccan harquebuses scattered and dropped so many of Songhai's forces that only the kneeling elite remained. Pasha Jawdar's army approached the elite of Songhai, still stuck in the kneeling pose. As they tore off the gold bands of the elite, the elite was heard shouting, "We are Muslims. Your brothers in religion!". Moroccans showed no mercy as they executed the remaining enemy elite (Garcia-Arenal, 2009, pg. 105).

Songhai suffered a crushing defeat at the hands of the Moroccan army in just one day (Ogot, 1992, pg. 154). Immediately after the horrendous battle, the inhabitants of Gao fled in frantically, many so flustered that they drowned crossing the Niger. As follows, the Askiya, his family, and the court took shelter on the right side of the river as well.

Ishaq II was defeated and nearly depleted. Jawdar, triumphant from battle, entered Gao, to his disappointment. There was no gold to be found in Gao, the capital of the empire. Their high hopes of Songhai's luxuriousness were a concept of western grandeur. He considered even the Askiya's house to be "primitive." The Pasha then attempted crossing the river by placing air-filled oxen hide under wooden rafts, but to no avail. Acknowledging his defeat, Askiya Ishaq II quickly offered a negotiation deal – 100,000 pieces of gold, 1,000 slaves, acknowledgment of Ahmad al-Mansur as Sultan, and control over the Taghaza salt mines that the al-Mansur attempted to take previously. In return, Ishaq wanted the immediate retreat of Jawdar and his men (Garcia-Arenal, 2009, pg. 105-6).

Pasha Jawdar thought the standing offer to be a good one. Also, he was concerned for the physical state of his men after the arduous voyage through the Sahara and the campaign at Tondibi. This encouraged him to relay the offer to his Sultan in Marrakesh (Ogot, 1992, pg. 154). The offer was sent with a gift of 200 slaves and 10,000 mithqals of gold. While awaiting the reply from Mulay Ahmad al-Mansur, Jawdar's men felt the effects of malaria and other illnesses in the area. Because of this, in April 1591, they entered Timbuktu in peace – at the same time Mansur received the letter relaying the offer of Ishaq II and the gifts. Mansur was angered and offended by the proposal of Ishaq and Jawdar. This angered him because Jawdar was so hasty to accept the deal and offended him because there was no prince sent from Songhai as a good-faith guarantee, as was customary for the Sudan. Jawdar was made to return the gifts, as Al-Mansur wanted Songhai banished and exiled from their own homelands (Garcia-Arenal, 2009, pg. 106).

By the end of June 1591, Pasha Mahmud ibn Zarqun, an additional Spanish renegade eunuch army general, with 40 men, was sent out by the Moroccan Sultan and arrived in Timbuktu in mid-August. Mahmud would be the replacement for the Jawdar. The orders were to take over Songhai by conquest to integrate it into the Moroccan Kingdom (Garcia-Arenal, 2009, pg. 107). Riches were sent back to Marrakesh by the Moroccans from the plunder and pillage of Timbuktu, Jenne, and Gao and dealt with the revolt of the Ulama (Islamic scholars) of Timbuktu. The remainder of Songhai army fled (Conrad, 2005, pg. 64). Chouki El Hamel points out: "Al-Ifrani stated that 'When Mahmud was in firm command of the situation there, he sent half of the army with a gift for al-Mansur. It contained untold treasures, including 1200 slaves, both male and female, forty loads of gold dust, four saddles of pure gold, many loads of ebony, a jar of galia, civet cats, and other highly-priced valuables.' As-Sa'di reported that al-Mansur was unsatisfied with the spoils of war. He proclaimed angrily his disappointment that his officers had amassed enormous wealth from the conquest but sent him only one hundred thousand mithqals (pieces of gold)" (2013, pg. 150).

The remaining Songhai army escaped to the rural countryside and substituted Askiya Ishaq II with his brother Muhammad Gao as the new Askiya. Ishaq tried to counter this but lost the support of his previously loyal subjects died soon after. The new Askiya wanted to make an offering of peace with the Moroccans in hopes of ending the conquest of Songhai territory. He was invited to visit with Pasha Mahmud ibn Zarqun. Little did Muhammad Gao know that this was an attempt at an ambush, which was successful. The new Askiya was slain on the spot, prematurely ending his short-lived reign (Conrad, 2005, pg. 64).

Songhai's rebellions ceased to stop as Askiya Sulyaman was placed on the throne by Mahmud as a puppet Askiya, but to no avail. The Songhai people did not accept or respect his authority. In return, they crowned their new king, Askiya Nuh, brother of Muhammad Gao, who continued the resistance of a rapidly dramatically declined empire (Conrad, 2005, pg. 64). The last stronghold was the Dendi province, which held firm resistance and started to possess firearms. After failing to take over Dendi, on September 27, 1593, he departed back to Timbuktu. Here he dealt with the agitated ulama issue, who had been revolting and letting their frustrations be known to the Moroccan Sultan about his soldier's barbarous nature (Kaba, 1981, pg. 469). In return, dozens of ulama were killed or sent to Morocco in exile, as they were held responsible for these uprisings in the mind of the Mahmud because he felt the ulama held sway over the Songhai. Among these ulama who was the famous Ahmad

Baba, who was boldly in opposition to the invasion of his nation (Hamel, 2012, pg. 150).

Internal conflicts within the Sa'adian army persisted, and so did Songhai resistance. In 1595, Ahmad al-Mansur began to question the success of Mahmud Pasha and sent a replacement, Mansur ibn Abd al-Rahman. This replacement was ordered to secretly arrest and murder Mahmud ibn Zarqun. Before this plan could be enacted, Mahmud received a "heads-up" from Abu Faris Abdallah, son of the Sultan al-Mansur and mentor to Mahmud. Mahmud left before his replacement arrived to attack archers in the mountains – this was against the figurehead Askiya Sulyaman's advice – and was killed in battle, January 1595. The sultan granted full administrative power to Jawdar Pasha. The result was a power struggle between the two. As al-Rahman began to reorganize the military and push against Askiya Nuh, he became unexpectedly ill, which caused him to return to Timbuktu, where he died in November of 1596. It is alleged that Jawdar murdered him via poison. This left Jawdar in charge as he wanted, all along. Mansur ibn Abd al-Rahman would not be the last Pasha to be sent by the Sultan, but most of them seemed to "mysteriously" meet a sudden death. Jawdar was finally recalled to Morocco in 1599 (Kaba,1981, pg. 470-1).

Though Askiya Nuh was able to hold off the Moroccan invaders until Jawdar's recall to Marrakesh, he was the first African ruler noted to use guerilla warfare tactics and win battles that Askiya Ishaq II failed to win (even with a larger army). By this time, the empire was greatly diminished and ceased to be the great Songhai from the time of Sunyi Ali and the past Askiyas. Though Jawdar was called back, Moroccans still occupied Timbuktu & Songhai urban areas; they later would become known as "Arma." David Conrad states: "With the great cities of the former Songhay Empire under Moroccan control, it did not take long for the formerly subjugated peoples to assert their independence and begin raiding one another. In the early 17th century, Tuareg nomads of the Sahara began making incursions into the great bend of the Niger River. The cattle-herding Fula of the Inland Delta formed their own state, called Masina, and began attacking their neighbors. Bamana warriors from upriver (southwest of Songhay) laid siege to Jenne and fought with the Fula. Armies from kingdoms in present-day northern Côte d'Ivoire and Burkina Faso also began advancing into southern regions of the former empire. By the 18th century, the former heartland of the Songhay Empire was occupied by several small states." (2005, pg. 64)

I conclude that the great Songhai empire was one of West Africa's most prized legacies. As the largest empire in West Africa's history, this chapter was not to praise the nation, as I am sure that this empire has no lack of veneration. My efforts were to show the causes of the death of Songhai as an Empire by the hands of the greedy Sultan of Morocco, and his Moroccan-Morisco & renegade army that would stay in the area, after all, is said & done, and later be known as the Arma people. Due to lack of technologically advanced weaponry, Mulay Ahmad al-Mansur was able to send a relatively small army to cross the dangerous Sahara – losing many soldiers on the journey – and into a land unfamiliar to them to dominate the battle of Tondibi and end it in a single day. Also, a big contribution to the downfall was the lack of preparation for the invading Moroccans. This is partly because Ishaq II did not believe that they would be able to cross the vicious Sahara intact and partly because of the disorganization due to struggles of succession to the seat of the throne. This had been an issue almost the entire duration of the Askiya dynasty, starting with Askiya Muhammad Ture being a usurper himself. The delusion of an "Islamic brotherhood" played a role as well. It was not thought that the ruler from an Islamic nation would militarily oppose the Askiyas, because that would be against Sharia (Islamic law) and all religious morality. The Blacks did not understand that these North Africans would use their religion to their advantage when possible and disregard its tenets when advantageous to them to do so. An eye-opening experience. As many of us are descendants of peoples of this prominent West African empire, we must never forget that we should continue to strive for technological advancement and not make the mistake of our ancestors in thinking tradition is always the best path, simply because its tradition.

The most beneficial way for those of recent African descent to advance is by science & technology. We must also stay reminded that if we are to use a religious system moving forward, that it should be a system with origins from us or our ancestors before us. Conversion to foreign religious systems is conversion to foreign cultural worldview.

We sometimes take these foreign systems more seriously and definitively those whom the culture is indigenous to. Hopefully, this chapter serves as a symbol of unification (not by the imaginary standards of every person of recent African descent are in agreement in every way to move forward), technological advancement, and rejection of foreign worldviews in any form.

Part V (culture)

SURVEY NINE

A Warrior-Scholar Examination and Assessment of African-American/African Biblical Religious belief via the use of Psychology, Sociology, Epistemology & Hermeneutics

Chavis Tp-hsb Ahaw McCray

A lot of people who have known me for longer than the past ten years have witnessed an intellectual maturity in the area of spirituality and religion that I believe has pushed some people away. I am not of the opinion that this distancing from some is the result of being personally offended or having a personal grudge. I am of the opinion that some people are willingly ignorant of historical realities and others only need religion to cope as a mechanism for them to deal with life, and in that information and knowledge that I came into creates cognitive dissonance and distortions for many. As I continue further in this chapter, I will define these terms like cognitive dissonance and cognitive distortion in an effort to offer edification as to where I am coming from with this analysis. I want to emphasize that these are not insults but strictly observations from a psychological perspective. But before I get into the assessment, I would like to offer personal insight as far as my past and how I came to the conclusions that I currently have drawn.

I didn't always question religion, the Bible, or God. For a long time, I considered myself a god-fearing Christian who just wanted to go to heaven and be like Jesus. My early memories of church are at Bella Vista Baptist Church in Studewood, a historic neighborhood in Houston's North (or Nawfside as we like to say down here in the 3rd coast), Where my Pawpaw was Deacon. It was the place where both sides of my family could be found on any given Sunday of the year. My parents were married there, and I was baptized there (2×) It's where we learned to pray and where we studied the Bible via Sunday School and Sunday sermons. I learned about the characters in The Bible by learning to memorize the books of the Bible, different verses of the Bible. We developed our morals around the Bible. We were disciplined based on the Bible. The Bible was where we drew from to obtain wisdom and understanding, and it was held in the highest regard. In our minds, it embodied the title of HOLY and was the tool with all the answers and guided us whether we were at Bella Vista or in San Diego at the San Diego Church of Christ (non-denominational) or a Baptist Church in San Diego or a Houston Church of Christ.

Bible and its God were the common denominators at any location. Especially since my dad was in the navy, and we went where he went, which happened to be San Diego, an entirely different environment than Houston. San Diego is extremely diverse compared to Houston especially depending on which areas you are in, but even in areas of poverty, there is a multitude of ethnicities in the city all over.

This being the case joining a non-denominational church that's multi-ethnic, you get an experience a little different from your Southern Baptist Church. The first thing you recognize is singing and the music and a difference in the way the Bible is interpreted essentially or more the delivery of sermons. Here, at this particular church in San Diego, not much zealous homily was expressed. There was more a focus on offering insightful positive life messages in what would Jesus do modern NIV bible reading sentiment versus old school Southern Baptist KJV reading paradigm. Both churches were essentially positive places for the members and help them deal with this thing we call life. My purpose and intent here is not to bad-mouth these establishments as they were foundational in my development in my adolescence.

However, I will objectively expose the reader to the realities of the psychology, historicity, and literary devices behind many ideas and concepts influenced by the book we call the Holy Bible and its contents. We also will objectively examine sociological dynamics associated with religious belief. To be completely honest, as a kid though going to church was a positive thing it was not where I personally wanted to spend my Sunday morning and afternoon. I, like others, basically was forced to continue to attend church all through my adolescence and teens. As a preteen, I started to question concepts in the Bible like who gets to go to heaven and who doesn't and why certain things were okay in the book, but other things weren't. I used to ask my mom where the native tribes, monks, Hindu people around the world who didn't know Jesus was going to hell, and she would tell me that basically, everyone will get a chance to know Jesus, and if they don't accept him, then they would perish basically. As a kid, I thought that was pretty messed up. An older Aunt who is now deceased by the name of Valerie used to question many of these ideas associated with the church in the Bible as well. At the church of Christ, there is a paradigm that once you are a certain age and you start dating that you stay inside the church as far as where you are to look for your mate.

My father and a lot of people look at the church as something of a cult. He preferred Baptist and was loyal to his church in Houston, bringing the family Bible from when he was married to San Diego, which was the King James version.

He used to make me memorize the books over and over and over until I could recite them all. When I wasn't doing that, I was in some type of workbook that my mom or the church gave me to study different parts of the Bible. My mom always gave me scriptures to read and have me go in the back of the book, look up other lessons, and search out the best scriptures that I can find, and I spend a lot of my time doing that. The older I got, the more I choose to utilize the book to deal with life and cope with everyday struggles. One thing I struggle with dealing with the Bible was separating what was literal and what was figurative. Certain parts of the Bible, like the parables of Jesus, were philosophical and could be interpreted in a lot of ways positively. But they were also parts that, if taken literally, I found disturbing and just automatically assume that they were not literal.

These logical conundrums were at the root of what pushed me away eventually from subscribing to that particular ideology viewing it in hindsight. It took me almost 27 years before I started critically examining things, I thought I knew. My journey wasn't a snap your fingers immediate transition; it was gradual. It's what Nipsey Hussle deemed a Marathon. For a long time, I avoided confrontational discussions regarding religious ideologies because I was taught not to question the Bible or God and not to lean on my own understanding through religious texts. For those who know me now know, I get a kick out of it. I think part of the reason why I avoided confrontation discussions on the topic is also because I wasn't really studied. I read the Bible from time to time but not enough.

The most I'd argue a person down was that God made marijuana, and they said it in the scripture he was cool with it. The first real passionate discussion I had in regards to the subject of Christianity was in 2011, maybe with my dad when he was in school taking philosophy. He was challenging my beliefs basically not intentionally but explaining to me what was going on in the classroom. I could not argue logically; I made countless appeals to emotion and incredulity. Maybe a year later, my roommate Desean came home one day awakened by some Hebrew Israelite knowledge and hit me with the question, when did the letter J originate. He stumped me because I had no clue. He started hitting me with the Jesus ain't real spill. All I could do to defend my belief was rationalize that the character in the story and tattoo on my forearm was a pretty good guy and never did anything wrong to anybody. So real or fake, he was cool with me because I didn't know for sure whether the guy was even real. I was indoctrinated. These were my first sign, and I had literally no clue. Sometime later, I watched a Kevin Wesley video that asked a question as to what nationality Jesus would have been and that basically he was a Jew, and I had never thought about that. That one question blew my mind because, as a Christian, we were taught to do what Jesus does, and for the first time in my life, I had to ask myself, okay, why are we Christians if he comes from a family of Jewish people. No one I got my Bible information from could answer that question preachers and all.

After getting that paradigm altering question from Kevin Wesley, I subscribe to his channel and end up hearing him mention Ray Hagins, who I eventually ended up following information-wise every day and learning about Maat and Kemet and contradictions and flaws in scripture. That was my beginning of becoming "woke" from there, I made the conscious decision to reprogram my mind and deal with knowledge over belief. I didn't know if saying in Jesus's name at the end of a prayer worked, so I stopped praying. I didn't want to believe anything from that point. I got invited to the Hebrew Israelite vs Kemetic group and started soaking game quietly gather resources through the group's members like Raheem and Marquez. I could tell they knew what they were talking about. That group led me to Sa Neter channel, watching Polight debates. I resonated most with the Amen Ra Squad scholarly method source up or shut up approach. All this was to build a foundation on objectivity, so my readers will know I came from thinking just like you. The only bias I have is against ignorance and tomfoolery. So, at this point, this is where I transition to how I got here in this book you are reading is being scholarly, and this is why KPRT made me a part of the team.

In previous volumes, you were educated on terms like religion, African traditional religion/systems, and historical documentation of Europeans and Arabs views of superiority over Africans. Going forward, the terms and concepts I introduce should add to that which you already have. I'll begin this quote from a book called The Rape of the Mind "The knowledge that the human mind can be influenced, tamed, and broken down into servility is far older than the modern dictatorial concept of enforced indoctrination. Throughout history, men have had an intuitive understanding that the mind can be manipulated. Elaborate strategies have been worked out to achieve this end. The continual intrusion into our minds of the hammering noises of arguments and propaganda can lead to two kinds of reactions. It may lead to apathy and indifference, the I-don't-care reaction, or to a more intensified desire to study and to understand."(Meerloo,1956)

"What we deem a religious education is characterized as religious indoctrination. Indoctrination is the process of inculcating a person with ideas, attitudes, cognitive strategies or professional methodologies."

(Snook, 1972)

A quick google search will inform you that it is "The process of teaching a person or group to accept a set of beliefs uncritically." (Oxford, n.d) Detaching myself emotionally from my journey knowledge-wise, that definition articulates exactly what took place. It isn't me trying to down any religion, simply the objective reality. I literally took everything in that book at face value. The very first few verses in the book demonstrate we as a collective people did uncritically accept this. The person supposedly writing Genesis was nowhere to be found if we are to take it seriously. To break this down quickly so far, we have a religious text and a religious ideology introduced to most African American people during slavery. "A dictionary defines sociology as the systematic study of society and social interaction. The word "sociology" is derived from the Latin word socius (companion) and the Greek word logos (speech or reason), which together mean "reasoned speech about companionship" (Little, n.d). Social scientists' approach is that religion exists as an organized and integrated set of beliefs, behaviors, and norms centered on basic social needs and values. Given the Bible was essentially a foreign religious text to the African has one ever pondered just exactly whose needs and values fuel these integrated beliefs, behavior, and norms.

People who are religious come from societies. Societies have culture. In that culture is where you'll find religious beliefs for people. In sociology, there are two terms non-material culture and material culture. (Little, n.d) Material culture would qualify as the Bible non-material would be the belief in Christianity One way to honestly explain the state of many black people who have uncritically accepted this material culture as an authority of any is via the term Deculturalization.

"Deculturalization is the process by which an ethnic group is forced to abandon its language, culture, and customs. It is the destruction of the culture of a minored group and its replacement by the culture of the dominating group" (Branch, 2014) Deculturalization is a slow process due to its extensive goal of entirely replacing the subordinate ethnic group's culture language, and customs. Methods of deculturization include:

- Geographical segregation
- Forbidding education to the dominated group
- Forceful replacing of language
- Superior culture's curriculum in schools
- Instructors are from the dominant group
- Avoiding the dominated group's culture in curriculum

Books like The Religious Instruction of the Negro offer a "historical sketch of the religious instruction of the negroes from their 1st introduction into the country in 1620 to the year 1842, divided into three periods."

The First Period — From their introduction in 1620 to the first century in 1790: a period of 170 years,

1. Account of the Introduction of NEGROES into the Colonies under the Government of Great Britain,

2. Estimated Negro Population of the Colonies at the Declaration of Independence and census of 1790,

3. Efforts for their Religious Instruction, both Great Britain and America, year by year, during this period,

The Second Period From the first census in 1790 to 1820: a period of 30 years, year by year, 47

The Third Period —From 1820 to 1842: a period of 22 years, year by year 1. Efforts year by year. Manual of instruction,

2. Action of Ecclesiastical Bodies, and different Denomination of Christians,

3. This period — a period of revival as to this particular duty, throughout the Southern States,

4. General Observations, in the conclusion of Historical Sketch,". (Jones, 1842)

This publication alone is historical documentation and support for evidence of methodically systemic deculturization imposed on the African. They don't teach you this at school, and you sure won't have a sermon about this on Sunday morning with your favorite preacher at the church you've been going to all your life. What I learned on this Marathon is people don't even know. They may have an idea, but many people have no clue about the actual evidence that exists to demonstrate the undeniable menticide and deculturization of the Africans. Your local preacher probably never read How to Make a Negro Christian, so I'm almost positive he wouldn't even know how to obtain the Religious Instruction of the Negro. Even if he did, he, like any other human being who subscribes to an ideology with such passion and emotion, only rationalizes and justifies the subscription's persistence.

From here, to make an assessment, we enter the mind utilizing studies of cognitive-behavioral psychology, epistemology, and anti-epistemology. "Anti-Epistemology is understood as the general process of covering and obscuring knowledge. We mean something more specific, namely an interesting phenomenon in the area of belief acquisition and revision. Sometimes people are very fond of certain beliefs. Prime examples are religious beliefs, but people may also cling to more mundane beliefs, such as the belief that they are morally decent persons or good drivers. Like most beliefs, these beliefs are linked to various other beliefs – other beliefs either confirm or disconfirm the original belief, support the original belief or call it into question. This can create a tension between the cherished belief and other beliefs, and the person may begin to feel cognitive dissonance." (Mannino, 2014)

Defining Cognitive dissonance, we find it "refers to a situation involving conflicting attitudes, beliefs or behaviors. This produces a feeling of mental discomfort leading to an alteration in one of the attitudes, beliefs or behaviors to reduce the discomfort and restore balance." (McLeod, 2018) Understanding that, we double back to anti epistemology and elaborate further, noting: "The idea of Anti-Epistemology revolves around three basic elements: the distinction between cherished beliefs and ordinary beliefs, the claim that beliefs are not isolated but stand in confirmation and disconfirmation relations to each other, and the idea that there are bad ways of resolving tension between beliefs and restoring rational equilibrium" (Mannino, 2014)

Knowing this, you have a better understanding behind the Dynamics of why there is rationalization and justification of this acceptance of the deculturalization. A person needs something to believe in to cope with reality comfortably. "All those opinions and notions of things, to which we have been accustomed from our infancy, take deep root, that 'tis impossible for us, by all powers of reason and experience, to eradicate them." Hume, A Treatise of Human Nature.

Most people are uncomfortable with what is called an etiological challenge. "An Etiological Challenge prompts the agent to assess whether her beliefs result from practices of indoctrination and whether she should reduce confidence in those beliefs. Given the anti-reliability of indoctrination as a method of belief-acquisition." (DiPaolo, J., Simpson, R.M, 2016), A response to the challenge usually results in belief perseverance which is described as " the tendency to cling to one's initial belief even after receiving new information that contradicts or disconfirms the basis of that belief. Everyone has tried to change someone's belief, only to have them stubbornly remain unchanged. " (Psychology, n.d) The backfire effect is a cognitive bias that causes people who encounter evidence that challenges their beliefs to reject that evidence and strengthen their support of their original stance. Essentially, the backfire effect means that showing people evidence that proves that they are wrong is often ineffective and can actually end up backfiring by causing them to support their original stance more strongly than they previously did. As such, the backfire effect is a subtype of the confirmation bias, which is a cognitive bias that can cause people to reject information that contradicts their beliefs or to interpret information in a way that confirms those beliefs (Effectiviology, n.d). Confirmation bias is "the tendency to process information by looking for, or interpreting, information that is consistent with one's existing beliefs. People are especially likely to process information to support their own beliefs when the issue is highly important or self-relevant." (Casad, n.d) Those who oppose my position argue that I am essentially doing the same I challenge those who oppose documents and demonstrate. As Ankh West says, "DON'T TALK ME TO DEATH," BECAUSE WE FOLLOW METHODOLOGY, EVIDENCE, AND TRUST SCIENCE and have no issue with proper correction based on sound evidence and logic.

Assessing these religious beliefs, one must begin to deal with the content and see what exactly these beliefs are to challenge them and why they should be challenged. For me, the Bible is simply goat herder of the middle east mythos now. My position is based on archaeological, biblical evidence, and current biblical scholarship. It is not a history book, but it does hold some historical value to some extent, depending on context and who you are speaking with. "Ahistoricism refers to a lack of concern for history, historical development, or tradition."(Mirriam-Webster Dictionary Online, 2008) Charges of historicism are frequently critical, implying that the subject is historically inaccurate or ignorant (for example, an ahistorical attitude). It can also describe a person's failure to frame an argument or issue in a historical context or to disregard historical fact or implication. (Pepper, 1993) Biblical narratives are constantly challenged from everything from the characters to who wrote the text, when they wrote it, what language they wrote it in. If you are Christian or Hebrew or Catholic or any subtype of an Abrahamic religion, have you asked yourself these questions? Have you done the work to support your belief and turn it into something you now know based on actual evidence? Or have you relied on faith and never challenge "God's word"? Well, today's your lucky day. I took the time to compile everything I could find scholastically that dealt with the historicity of the Bible from my journey with sources attached.

"In the following decades, Hermann Gunkel drew attention to the mythic aspects of the Pentateuch. Albrecht Alt, Martin Noth, and the traditional history school argued that although its core traditions had genuinely ancient roots. The narratives were fictional framing devices and were not intended as history in the modern sense. Though doubts have been cast on the historiographic reconstructions of this school (particularly the notion of oral traditions as a primary ancient source), much of its critique of biblical historicity found wide acceptance. Gunkel's position is that if we consider figures like Abraham, Isaac, and Jacob to be actual persons with no original mythic foundations, that does not mean that they are historical figures. ...For even if, as may well be assumed, there was once a man-call "Abraham," everyone who knows the history of legends is sure that the legend is in no position at the distance of so many centuries to preserve a picture of the personal piety of Abraham. The "religion of Abraham" is, in reality, the religion of the legend narrators which they attribute to Abraham."1. (Gunkel 1997, p. lxviii)

"In the United States, the biblical archaeology movement, under the influence of Albright, counterattacked, arguing that the broad outline within the framing narratives was also true, so that while scholars could not realistically expect to prove or disprove individual episodes from the life of Abraham and the other patriarchs. These were real individuals who could be placed in a context proven from the archaeological record. But as more discoveries were made and anticipated finds failed to materialize, it became apparent that archaeology did not in fact support the claims made by Albright and his followers. Today, only a minority of scholars continue to work within this framework, mainly for reasons of religious conviction." (Mazar, Amihay Archaeology of the land of the Bible, 10,000-586 BCE. Garden City, NY: Doubleday. ISBN 978-0385425902. 1992)

BIBLICAL HISTORY AND ISRAEL'S PAST

The Changing Views of Scholars in Their Own Words The dramatic shifts in the study of the patriarchs and matriarchs that occurred during and after the 1970s can be illustrated by quotations from two works on the history of Israel separated by several decades. In a history originally written in the 1950s, John Bright asserted, "Abraham, Isaac, and Jacob were clan chiefs who lived in the second millennium BC. The Bible's narrative accurately reflects the times to which it refers. But to what it tells of the lives of the patriarchs, we can add nothing."1 Assessing the situation in scholarship four decades later, William Dever, in 2001, concluded, "After a century of exhaustive investigation, all respectable archaeologists have given up hope of recovering any context that would make Abraham, Isaac, or Jacob credible 'historical figures.'"2 1. John Bright, A History of Israel, 4th ed. (Louisville: Westminster John Knox, 2000), p. 93. 2. William G. Dever, What Did the Biblical Writers Know, and When Did They Know It? What Archaeology Can Tell Us About the Reality of Ancient Israel (Grand Rapids: Eerdmans, 2001), p. 98.

"Historical figures but as literary creations of this later period. Though the evidentiary underpinnings of this thesis were new, the thesis itself was quite similar to the views held by Alt and Noth. Thompson, Van Seters, and others had shown that the earlier scholarly consensus of a second-millennium date for the traditions depended upon coincidences and harmonization of evidence that could not be sustained. Thompson provided one of the most representative statements of this change in the study of Israel's past: "[N]ot only has 'archaeology' not proven a single event of the patriarchal traditions to be historical, it has not shown any of the traditions to be likely. Based on what we know of the Palestinian history of the Second Millennium BC, and of what we understand about the formation of the literary traditions of Genesis, it must be concluded that any such historicity as is commonly spoken of in both scholarly and popular works about the patriarchs of Genesis is hardly possible and totally improbable."

Bibliography

Survey One

DINKA --PEOPLE: THE GREAT CATTLE HERDERS OF SUDAN, Blogger, 5 Nov. 2013, kwekudee-tripdownmemorylane.blogspot.com/2012/10/dinka-people-great-cattle-herders-of.html.

Asante , Molefi Kente, and Ama Mazama . Encyclopedia of African Religion. SAGE, 2009.

Fisher, Angela, and Carol Beckwith. Dinka: Legendary Cattle Keepers of Sudan. Rizzoli, 2010.

Ryle, John. Warrior of the White Nile. Time-Life Books, 1982.

Survey Two

"The Lost Boys of Sudan." International Rescue Committee (IRC), International Rescue Committee (IRC), October 3 2014, www.rescue.org/article/lost-boys-sudan?amp.

Wama, Barnabas L. Prolonged Wars: the War in Sudan. Biblioscholar, 2012.

Jal, Emmanuel, and Megan Lloyd-Davies. War Child: a Child Soldier's Story. St. Martin's Press, 2010.

"Sudan: American Resettlement of "Lost Boys" Continues". Reliefweb. OCHA. Retrieved June 21, 2018.

Bixler, Mark. The Lost Boys of SUDAN: An American Story of the Refugee Experience. University of Georgia Press, 2006.

Survey Three

Evans, Alistair-Boddy. Biography of John Garang De Mabior Leader and Founder of the Sudan People's Liberation Army. n.d..

Garang, John. John Garang Speaks: The Call for Democracy in Sudan. Kegan Paul International, 1990.

Johnson, D. The Root Causes of Sudan's Civil Wars, Indiana University Press, 2003, pp. 61–2.

"Leaders call death of former rebel leader a great loss to Sudan". The New York Times. August 2, 2005. Retrieved November 19, 2018.

Samms, Andrew. "The South Sudanese Civil War (2013-) •." •, 19 Jan. 2021, www.blackpast.org/global-african-history/south-sudanese-civil-war-2013/.

Survey Four

Shaolin Kung Fu Academy for Shaolin Temple Wushu School China, Shaolin Temple. "Welcome to Shaolin Temple Kung Fu Academy China." China Shaolin Kungfu Academy, 2020, shaolinacademy.net/.

School, Shaolin Temple Tagou Wushu. "Kung Fu Styles at Shaolin Tagou Wushu School." Shaolin Tagou Martial Arts

School, Shaolin Tagou Martial Arts School, 2021, www.shaolintagou.org/training/shaolin-kung-fu-styles/.

Zhouxiang, Dr Lu. "Column: The History, Politics and Identity of Chinese Martial Arts." TheJournal.ie, Journal Media Limited, 2021, www.thejournal.ie/readme/history-and-politics-chinese-martial-arts-5449729-Jun2021/.

Yongxin, Sifu Shi. "Five Animals of Gong Fu." Shaolin.org.cn, 2021, www.shaolin.org/general-3/research/shaolin-five-animals/five-animals01.html.

Sephyx, Milly. "Top 10 Facts about the Maasai People of Kenya." Discover Walks Blog, Charing Cross Corporation, 14 Jan. 2021, www.discoverwalks.com/blog/nairobi/top-10-facts-about-the-maasai-people-of-kenya/.

History , Militria. "Weapons of the Zulu." Militaria History, Warners Group Publications, 20 Jan. 2020, www.militaria-history.co.uk/articles/weapons-of-the-zulu/.

Safaris, AJ Kenya. "The Maasai People - Culture, HIstory and Facts." AjKenyaSafaris, AJ Kenya Safaris, 8 Dec. 2020, ajkenyasafaris.com/maasai-people/.

Survey Five

Nordquist, Richard. "Learn the Function of Code Switching as a Linguistic Term." ThoughtCo, Dec. 27, 2020, thoughtco.com/code-switching-language-1689858.

Cole, Nicki Lisa, Ph.D. "Understanding Acculturation and Why It Happens." ThoughtCo, Dec. 30, 2020, thoughtco.com/acculturation-definition-3026039.

Waring, Chandra. "What Is Code-Switching and Why Do Black Americans Do It?", August 17, 2018

Hua, Z. "Duelling Languages, Duelling Values: Codeswitching in bilingual intergenerational conflict talk in diasporic families" February 2008

Shariatmadari,D. "The Limits of Standard English"January 7, 2020

Webb. V, Sure. "African Voices: An Introduction to the Languages of Africa".Oxford 2000 Imhotep, A "Nsw.t Bjt.j (king) in Ancient Egyptian: A Lesson in Paronymy and Leadership" Madu Ndela Press 2016

Wilson, A. "The Developmental Psychology of the Black Child" AfrikanWorld Info systems 2014

Survey Six

Cartwright, Mark. "Surya." World History Encyclopedia, World History Encyclopedia, 26 June 2021, www.worldhistory.org/Surya/#ci_related_filters=type:0&page:2.

History.com Editors. "Hunter-Gatherers." History.com, A&E Television Networks, 5 Jan. 2018, www.history.com/topics/pre-history/hunter-gatherers.

Maestri, Nicoletta. "Chalchiuhtlicue: Aztec Water Goddess and Sister of the Rain God Tlaloc." ThoughtCo, www.thoughtco.com/chalchiuhtlicue-goddess-170327.

The Maya and the Sun Images used in this video can be downloaded in the Resources Section of the site. Download PDF trans. "The Maya and the Sun." - Sun, Corn and the Calendar, maya.nmai.si.edu/maya-sun/maya-and-sun.

Minster, Christopher. "The Mighty Sun God of the Inca." ThoughtCo, www.thoughtco.com/inti-the-inca-sun-god-2136316.

Nnadiebube Journal of Philosophy (NJP), nigerianjournalsonline.com/index.php/NJP.

Storm, Rachel. Mythology of Egypt and the Middle East: Myths and Legends of Egypt, Persia, Asia Minor, Sumer and Babylon. Southwater, 2007.

Survey Seven

Ade, Ajayi Jacob Festus, and Michael Crowder. History of West Africa. Volume One. Vol. 1, Longman, 1976.

Crowder, Michael. West Africa: an Introduction to Its History. Longman, 1990.

Gomez, Michael A. African Dominion: a New History of Empire in Early and Medieval West Africa. Princeton University Press, 2019.

Insoll, Timothy. The Archaeology of Islam in Sub-Saharan Africa. Cambridge University Press, 2003.

Ki-Zerbo, Joseph, et al. General History of Africa. Abridged ed., IV, Heinemann, 1997.

Kutī, Timbuktī, Maḥmūd Kutī ibn Mutawakkil, et al. The Timbuktu Chronicles, 1493-1599: English Translation of the Original Works in Arabic by Al Hajj Mahmud Kati. Africa World Press, 2011.

'Abdallāh As-Sa'dī 'Abd ar-Raḥmān Ibn, and John O. Hunwick. Timbuktu and the Songhay Empire: Al-Sa'dī's Ta'rīkh Al-sūdān down to 1613 and Other Contemporary Documents. Brill, 2003.

Saad, Elias N. Social History of Timbuktu: the Role of Muslim Scholars and Notables, 1400-1900. Cambridge University Press, 2010.

Survey Eight

Bovill, E. W. (1958). The Golden Trade Of The Moors. Markus Wiener Publishers.

Empires of Medieval West Africa (Great Empires of the Past) by Tbd/Shoreline Publishing (2005–05-01). (2005). Facts on File (2005–05-01).

Garcia-Arenal, M. (2009). Ahmad al-Mansur: The Beginnings of Modern Morocco (Makers of the Muslim World). Oneworld Academic.

Hamel, C. E. (2013). Black Morocco: A History of Slavery, Race, and Islam (African Studies) by Chouki El Hamel(2008–07-06). Cambridge University Press.

Holst, C. (2016). Muslim Traders, Songhay Warriors and the Arma: The Social Destruction of the Middle Niger Bend from 1549 to 1660. n/a.

Hunwick, J. O. (2003). Timbuktu and the Songhay Empire: Al-Sa'Di's Ta'Rikh Al-Sudan Down to 1613 and Other Contemporary Documents. Brill Academic Pub.

Kaba, L. (1981). Archers, Musketeers, and Mosquitoes: The Moroccan Invasion of the Sudan and the Songhay Resistance (1591–1612). The Journal of African History, 22(4), 457–475. https://doi.org/10.1017/s0021853700019861

Ogot, B. A. (1992). General History of Africa volume 5: Africa from the 16th to the 18th Century (Unesco General History of Africa (abridged)). James Currey.

Williams, C. (1971). THE DESTRUCTION OF BLACK CIVILIZATION GREAT ISSUES OF A RACE FROM 4500 B .C. TO 2000 A .D . Third World Press.

Survey Nine

Meerloo, J. A. M. (1956). The rape of the mind: The psychology of thought control, menticide, and brainwashing. The World Publishing Company. https://doi.org/10.1037/13187-000

Thiessen, E.J. Indoctrination and religious education. Interchange 15, 27–43 (1984). https://doi.org/10.1007/BF01807940

Funk and Wagnalls: "To instruct in doctrines; esp., to teach partisan or sectarian dogmas"; IA Snook, ed. 1972. Concepts of Indoctrination (London: Routledge and Kegan Paul).

Little, W. (n.d.) Introduction to sociology - 1st Canadian edition. BC. Open Textbook project. https://opentextbc.ca/introductiontosociology/front-matter/about-the-book/

Branch, André J. "Deculturalization". SAGE knowledge. SAGE Publications, Inc. Retrieved 9 November 2014.

Jones, Charles Colcock, 1804-1863 "The Religious Instruction of the Negroes." In the United States:Electronic Edition.

Meerloo, J. A. M. (1956). The rape of the mind: The psychology of thought control, menticide, and brainwashing. The World Publishing Company. https://doi.org/10.1037/13187-000

Thiessen, E.J. Indoctrination and religious education. Interchange 15, 27–43 (1984). https://doi.org/10.1007/BF01807940

Funk and Wagnalls: "To instruct in doctrines; esp., to teach partisan or sectarian dogmas"; I.A. Snook, ed. 1972. Concepts of Indoctrination (London: Routledge and Kegan Paul).

Little, W. (n.d.) Introduction to sociology - 1st Canadian edition. B.C. Open Textbook project. https://opentextbc.ca/introductiontosociology/front-matter/about-the-book/

Branch, André J. "Deculturalization". SAGE knowledge. SAGE Publications, Inc. Retrieved 9 November 2014.

Jones, Charles Colcock, 1804-1863 "The Religious Instruction of the Negroes." In the United States:Electronic Edition.

Anti-Epistemology 2nd November 2014,written by Adriano Mannino http://crucialconsiderations.org/rationality/anti-epistemology/Cognitive Dissonance By Saul McLeod, updated Feb 05, 2018 https://www.simplypsychology.org/cognitive-dissonance.html

DiPaolo, J., Simpson, R.M. Indoctrination anxiety and the etiology of belief. Synthese 193, 3079–3098 (2016). https://doi.org/10.1007/s11229-015-0919-6 (Psychology, n.d) https://psychology.iresearchnet.com/social-psychology/social-cognition/belief-perseverance/(Effectiviology, n.d) https://effectiviology.com/backfire-effect-facts-dont-change-minds/

Pepper, David (1993). Eco-socialism: From Deep Ecology to Social Justice. Routledge. pp. 143–144. ISBN 978-William Grassie, 2012 "The Sciences of Sacred Scriptures" https://m.huffpost.com/us/entry/us_1244745

Available now!!!

Available now!!!

Available now!!!

Available now!!!

Available now!!!

Available now!!!

Available now!!!

Available now!!!

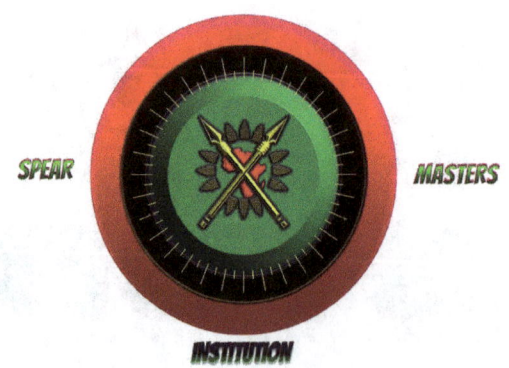

www.ingramcontent.com/pod-product-compliance
Lightning Source LLC
Chambersburg PA
CBHW051925160426
43198CB00012B/2048